WORLD KITCHEN
SPAIN

WORLD KITCHEN
SPAIN

MURDOCH BOOKS

CONTENTS

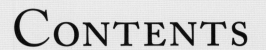

THE THREE MAJOR INFLUENCES ON THE CUISINE OF A COUNTRY ARE ITS GEOGRAPHY, ITS HISTORY AND ITS PERSONALITY. NOWHERE IS THIS MORE CLEARLY SEEN THAN IN THE FOOD OF SPAIN.

The Iberian Peninsula, comprising both Spain and Portugal, stretches from southern France to northern Africa, from which continent it is separated by only a sliver of the Mediterranean at the Straits of Gibraltar. Contained in its 640 square kilometres is the most varied range of landscapes in all of Europe. The Sierra Nevada is snow-capped all year round, yet at its feet lies an almost tropical coast. Spain has the highest mean altitude of any country in Europe but Switzerland – about 40 per cent of it is highland plateau, a windswept treeless meseta (high central plain), blasted by the sun in summer and the snows of winter.

To the north and north-west, bordering the Atlantic, is green Spain: mists and mountains; high rainfall; and lush forests. Also in the north, in the province of Asturias, are the Picos de Europa, three towering massifs, separated from one another by steep gorges, a mountain range that stretches

to within 15 kilometres of the Cantabrian coast, a coast that offers almost Scandinavian peaks and valleys, and rivers teeming with salmon and trout. To the south, the chalky soil of Jerez de la Frontera is inland, with the coastline stretching to contain the Donaña National Park, sandy woodlands that shelter red deer and a wilderness of wetlands. In the province of Almeria, in the far south-eastern corner of the country, is Europe's only desert and the location for the filming of many of Spain's 'paella' westerns.

Then there are Spain's two island groups. First, the Balearic Islands, near the eastern coast of the peninsula: mountainous Mallorca, gently rolling Menorca, pine-clad (and tourist-wracked) Ibiza and almost barren Formentera. South and west, closer to Africa than to the peninsula, and a remnant of the age of empires, are the seven islands of the Canaries, each boasting its own unique natural features.

This immensely varied landscape is home to an equally wide variety of produce and livestock, and a multitude of seafood in the waters that lap Spain's shores, from the Mediterranean to the Atlantic Ocean and the Cantabrian Sea.

Is it any wonder that such a strategically placed and geographically diverse country has been subjected to so many invasions over the centuries? First came the Phoenicians, then the Carthaginians, the Greeks, the Romans, the Visigoths and Moors. Beginning in the 700s, originally with the Berber tribesmen from north Africa and then the Arabs from as far afield as Syria, the Moors ruled for nearly 800 years. Each group left a different culinary imprint on the land. The Phoenicians brought olive trees, although it was the Romans and later the Moors who began their widespread cultivation. The Romans also brought different methods of cooking (roasting and grilling), the first cereals and introduced bread and baking.

After the Romans came the Visigoths, who were responsible for developing livestock farming, and, one could speculate, helping develop the cheese making that today flourishes in the provinces of Asturias, and Castile and León. The Visigoths also

introduced legumes and vegetables from northern Europe, including spinach and radishes, that were well suited to the Spanish soil. Another benefit of the Germanic invasions was exposure to medieval cuisines from the north.

But no peoples left more of a mark on the food, or the culture, of Spain than the Moors. For them, Al-Andalus (the Arabic name the Moors used to refer to the parts of the Iberian Peninsula under their control) was an earthly paradise, even more so once they had developed its agriculture, transforming large areas of arid land into green and well-watered oases using gravity flow canals and waterwheels.

Once the land had been tamed, the Moors then introduced an astonishing variety of produce. Citrus, including sour (later Sevilla) oranges, lemons and limes; apricots, bananas and almonds; from Asia came rice, taro and sugar cane, the rice planted in the river deltas of the Levante in the province of Valencia. Then the vegetables, among them artichokes, eggplant (aubergine), celery, spinach and carrots. Perhaps most important of all, the Moors contributed hard wheat, Triticum durum, from which pasta was made.

At the height of its power, around the mid-tenth century, Islamic Spain was the intellectual and scientific centre of the world, its capital Córdoba described as 'the ornament of the world'. Arab, Jew and Christian lived, for the greater part of their rule, side by side in harmony.

It was only after 1492, when the last Moorish stronghold in Granada fell and Spain was reunified, that Spanish food took the shapes we recognize today. The importation from the New World of those strange, new and, at first, suspicious foods – the tomato, the potato, the capsicum (pepper), the chilli and chocolate – contributed to the unique, hybrid nature of Spanish cuisine.

The last of these three great influences on Spanish cuisine, after geography and history, is perhaps

the most important: the personality of the peoples cooking the food. It should be remembered that Spain is a political construct, made up of several distinct groups, many with their own languages. There are the Basques, whose lands are in the north-east, along a porous border with France (there are French as well as Spanish Basques); to their west, the Galicians; south and east the Catalans and Valencians; off the shores of these two provinces the Balearic Islands, holding the Mallorquins, Menorcans and Ibicencans (natives of Ibiza), all of whom speak a variation of the Catalan language. Then there are the Asturians, Andalucíans, Extremadurans, and the Navarrans, all of whom have their own cuisines, their own ingredients, shaped by their geography, their history, and their personality.

Two traditions emphasize this point and the vast differences you will find as you move throughout the Iberian Peninsula. In the Basque country, there is an ancient tradition of gentlemen's cooking clubs. At the end of a hard day's work, Basque men will go to their clubs and, on a roster system, cook elaborate meals for their fellow members. Banker, doctor and plumber down tools and pick up pans to prepare these meals together. The Basques are well known for their love of food – and this shines through in their dishes and the star-studded restaurants of their capital, San Sebastián. And no wonder – they have access to such wonderful produce: draw a circle 100 kilometres around San Sebastián, and you will find the best seafood in Spain, the vegetables of Navarra, foie gras from the Landes, and the truffles of the Perigord.

At the other end of the spectrum is the phenomena of la nueva cocina, directly translated as 'the new cooking of Spain', whose most famous exponent is a Catalan, Ferran Adrià. The Catalans, the Spanish will tell you, are astute and creative. These traits most definitely apply to Adrià. He has marketed his restaurant on the Costa Brava and himself ingeniously; his cuisine is as creative in its way as the output of that other famous Catalan artist, Salvador Dali, with whom he is often compared. Adrià is not the only exponent of the new cooking of Spain, but he is one of the few many remember because of his audacious culinary inventions, first among them the 'foams' (or espuma), created by aerating the main ingredient and air. And yet as inventive as Adrià's food is, with a sense of humour and a dash of irony, at heart it is still Spanish food. As Adrià himself has said, 'you cook where you find yourself, and I find myself in Spain'.

With an abundance of fresh produce, seafood, meat, spices and herbs from around the world, this cuisine is nothing if not a fantastic amalgamation of some of the best tastes and flavours available.

Although this book does touch on some of the more modern interpretations of classic Spanish recipes, it will not explore the intricacies of la nueva cocina, the new cooking of Spain. It serves instead to provide a collection of traditional Spanish recipes along with others inspired by the spirit and the ingredients of the Spanish kitchen.

With an abundance of fresh produce, seafood, meat, spices and herbs from around the world, this cuisine is nothing if not a fantastic amalgamation of some of the best tastes and flavours available. These recipes feature some of the more traditional of the Spanish ingredients: olives and the oil they produce, from the mild, light oils to the heavier, richer varieties; sherry, fine and light, or of a darker hue with a richer flavour and texture; bacalao, popular in the Basque country, and which, if it is cured and prepared properly, will emerge smooth, firm and white, with a hint of the salt it has been preserved in; fresh seafood, plucked directly from the oceans surrounding the Iberian Peninsula; rice, brought by the Moors and used extensively throughout the country, most popularly in the ubiquitous paella; jamón, at its best when served simply, with no garnish to detract from the subtle combination of its flesh and fat; the wine, making its presence known on the wine scene with a rich,

fresh outlook; and finally, the cheese, beloved by Spanish people and a highlight of any venture into a tapas bar.

Some traditions hold Spain together more than any political directives from Madrid. Because the Spanish universally do not start their evening meal until late – often as late as 11 pm – they take tapas to stave off the pangs of hunger. The average Anglo Saxon stomach visiting Spain for the first time will have to adjust to this Spanish eating schedule: if it is accustomed to being lined between seven and eight every evening, it will have to wind its gastric clock back at least two hours. Late for everything else, the Spanish are habitually late for the evening meal – hence the success of tapas. From Malaga to Palma de Mallorca, from Barcelona to Badajoz, you will find this tradition of bar hopping and feasting on tiny plates.

And there you have it. The food of Spain, like the land itself, from mountain tops to its long stretches of beach, straddles great culinary distances, from the slow-roasted suckling lamb of Segovia to the humble tortilla de patatas found in every bar in the land all the way to the wilder shores of the intricate molecular gastronomy of la nueva cocina.

And so, as they say in Spain, buen provecho!

Chapter 1

THE TAPAS BAR

The innkeepers of Andalucía were the first to hand out free snacks with the evening glass of chilled sherry or wine, beginning the wonderful tradition of tapas.

TORTILLA

Potato Omelette

Such a simple dish, so difficult to perfect. A tortilla must be light, the potato firm, the onions ever so slightly caramelized, and the eggs cooked enough to hold the whole dish together but no more. The tortilla is the dish by which to judge a tapas bar.

500 g (1 lb 2 oz) all-purpose potatoes, peeled and
   cut into 1 cm (½ in) slices
60 ml (2 fl oz/¼ cup) olive oil
1 brown onion, thinly sliced

4 garlic cloves, thinly sliced
2 tablespoons finely chopped flat-leaf (Italian) parsley
6 eggs

Put the potato slices in a large saucepan, cover with cold water and bring to the boil over high heat. Boil for 5 minutes, then drain and set aside.

Heat the oil in a deep-sided non-stick frying pan over medium heat. Add the onion and garlic and cook for 5 minutes, or until the onion softens.

Add the potato and parsley to the pan and stir to combine. Cook over medium heat for 5 minutes, gently pressing down into the pan.

Whisk the eggs with 1 teaspoon each of salt and freshly ground black pepper and pour evenly over the potato. Cover and cook over low–medium heat for 20 minutes, or until the eggs are just set. Slide onto a serving plate or serve directly from the pan.

SERVES 6–8

Gently press down on the potato, onion, garlic and parsley combination as it cooks to help compact it.

ALCACHOFAS EN VINAGRETA AROMÁTICA

Artichokes in Vinaigrette

This tapa, based on the globe artichoke in a delicious aromatic vinaigrette, comes with its own handle, the stalk. Artichokes were first introduced into Spain by the Moors in the mid-fifteenth century, and their use often reflects this rich heritage.

2 tablespoons lemon juice
4 large globe artichokes
2 garlic cloves, crushed
1 teaspoon finely chopped oregano
½ teaspoon ground cumin

½ teaspoon ground coriander
pinch of chilli flakes
3 teaspoons sherry vinegar
60 ml (2 fl oz/¼ cup) olive oil

Add the lemon juice to a large bowl of cold water, forming what is known as acidulated water. Trim the artichokes, cutting off the stalks to within 5 cm (2 in) of the base of each artichoke and removing all the tough outer leaves. Cut off the top quarter of the leaves from each. Slice each artichoke in half from the top to base, or into quarters if large. Remove each small, furry choke with a teaspoon, then place each artichoke in the bowl of acidulated water to prevent it from discolouring while you prepare the rest.

Bring a large non-aluminium saucepan of water to the boil, add the artichokes and 1 teaspoon of salt and simmer for 20 minutes, or until tender. (The cooking time will depend on the artichoke size.) Test by pressing a skewer into the base. If cooked,

the artichoke will be soft and give little resistance. Strain, then drain the artichokes on their cut side while cooling.

Combine the garlic, oregano, cumin, coriander and chilli flakes in a small bowl. Season with salt and pepper and blend in the sherry vinegar. Beating constantly, slowly pour in the olive oil to form an emulsion. This step can also be done in a small food processor.

Arrange the artichokes in rows on a serving platter. Pour the dressing over the top and leave to cool completely.

SERVES 4

Using a small spoon, scoop out the fibrous, indigestible artichoke hearts.

FLAMENQUINES CORDOBESES
Cordoban Pork Rolls

These pork rolls are a specialty of the city of Córdoba, in Andalucía. They are called flamenquines after the Flemish soldiers who accompanied Emperor Carlos V – the soldiers were blond, much like the coating of beaten egg in the dish.

100 g (4 oz) butter
60 g (2 oz/½ cup) plain (all-purpose) flour
185 ml (6 fl oz/¾ cup) milk
185 ml (6 fl oz/¾ cup) chicken stock
4 pork schnitzel pieces, 100 g (4 oz) each
4 thin slices jamón, 100 g (4 oz) each
2 tablespoons finely chopped flat-leaf (Italian) parsley

2 garlic cloves, finely chopped
2 large eggs
dash of milk
plain (all-purpose) flour, for coating
dried breadcrumbs, for coating
olive oil, for deep-frying

In a saucepan, melt the butter over low–medium heat. Add the flour and cook for 1–2 minutes, stirring. Slowly whisk in the combined milk and stock mixture. Season and stir for 8–10 minutes, or until quite thick. Cool to room temperature, then cover and refrigerate until well chilled.

Using a mallet, pound the pork until about 5 mm (¼ in) thick and slightly longer and wider than the jamón slices. Trim the edges to form rectangles.

Lay a piece of jamón over the top of each rectangle. Combine the parsley and garlic and sprinkle on top. Roll up and hold in place with a toothpick. Refrigerate until ready to use.

When the white sauce is cold and firm, remove it from the refrigerator. You will need to mould the sauce around the pork. Add a little milk if the mixture won't stick to the pork. Note that it is important to work quickly – the mixture just needs to coat the pork, it doesn't need to look too neat as the pork will be coated in crumbs. Place on a tray in a single layer, then cover and refrigerate for 1 hour to firm up again.

Combine the eggs with a dash of milk in a bowl. Place the flour and breadcrumbs on separate plates. Lightly coat the pork rolls in the flour, then dip into the egg wash and lift out, allowing any excess to drip off. Roll in the breadcrumbs. Refrigerate until ready to cook to firm the crumbs. Preheat the oven to 180°C (350°F/Gas 4).

Meanwhile fill a deep-fryer or a heavy-based saucepan one-third full of oil and heat the oil to 180°C (350°F), or until a cube of bread dropped into the oil browns in 15 seconds. Fry the pork for about 1 minute on each side, or until golden. Transfer to the oven for 15–20 minutes, or until firm to touch. Remove the toothpicks and serve.

SERVES 4–6

CALAMARES FRITOS

Fried Calamari

No other tapa, with the exception of the tortilla and Russian salad, can be seen in tapas bars from Jerez de la Frontera to Santiago de Compostela. Fried calamari (squid) on the menu is a perfect barometer of a good tasca, Spanish bar or gathering place.

500 g (1 lb 2 oz) cleaned squid tubes
185 g (7 oz/1½ cups) plain (all-purpose) flour
2 teaspoons sweet paprika (pimentón)

olive oil, for deep-frying
lemon wedges, to serve
allioli (see page 249), to serve (optional)

Wash the calamari and cut into rings 1 cm (½ in) wide. Combine the flour and paprika. Season the calamari rings well with salt and pepper and toss in the flour to lightly coat.

Fill a deep, heavy-based saucepan one-third full of olive oil and heat to 180°C (350°F), or until a cube of bread dropped into the oil browns in 15 seconds. Cook the calamari rings in batches for 2 minutes, or until golden. Drain and serve hot with lemon wedges and allioli if desired.

SERVES 4–6

SANGRIA

Red Wine Punch

1½ tablespoons caster (superfine) sugar
1 tablespoon lemon juice
1 tablespoon fresh orange juice
750 ml (26 fl oz) bottle of red wine
  (preferably Spanish)
500 ml (17 fl oz/2 cups) lemonade

2 tablespoons gin
2 tablespoons vodka
1 lemon
1 orange
1 lime
ice cubes, to fill pitcher

Put the caster sugar, lemon juice and orange juice in a large pitcher or bowl and stir until the sugar has dissolved. Add the red wine, lemonade, gin and vodka.

Cut the lemon, orange and lime into halves, remove the seeds and slice all the fruit thinly. Add the slices to the pitcher and fill with the ice cubes. Stir well.

SERVES 10

BOCADILLOS

Little Sandwiches

The bocadillo has humble beginnings, originally a working-class answer to the merienda, the light snack many Spaniards eat to tide them over until their main evening meal. Now anyone can enjoy a bocadillo as a tasty treat at any time of the day.

6 mini crispy bread rolls
90 g (3 oz/⅓ cup) allioli (see page 249)
12 slices jamón or prosciutto

300 g (11 oz) pimiento de picillo, cut into strips
150 g (6 oz) Manchego cheese, thinly sliced

Cut open the bread rolls with a bread knife, leaving them hinged, then spread each bread roll with some of the allioli.

Put two slices of jamón on top of the allioli, followed by some strips of pimiento and slices of Manchego. Serve immediately.

MAKES 6

GAMBAS AL AJILLO

Garlic Prawns

As an appetizer for a dinner party, or one of the many tapas you tuck in to over a glass of wine and some good conversation, this dish is sure to be a hit. Serve in cazuelas de barro (earthenware ramekins) for a particularly authentic approach.

1.25 kg (2 lb 12 oz) raw prawns (shrimp)
80 g (3 oz) butter, melted
185 ml (6 fl oz/¾ cup) olive oil

8 garlic cloves, crushed
2 spring onions (scallions), thinly sliced
crusty bread, to serve

Preheat the oven to 250°C (500°F/Gas 9). Peel the prawns, leaving the tails intact. Pull out the vein from the back, starting at the head end. Cut a slit down the back of each prawn.

Combine the butter and oil and divide among four 500 ml (17 fl oz/2 cup) cast-iron pots. Divide half the crushed garlic among the pots.

Place the pots on a baking tray and heat in the oven for 10 minutes, or until the mixture is bubbling. Remove from the oven and divide the prawns and remaining garlic among the pots. Return to the oven for 5 minutes, or until the prawns are cooked. Stir in the spring onion. Season to taste. Serve with bread to mop up the juices.

PICTURE ON PAGE 24

SERVES 4

Garlic Prawns (recipe on page 23)

HABAS CON JAMÓN
Broad Beans with Jamón

The Spanish love their vegetables – especially pulses. They particularly love to combine vegetables with the saltiness of jamón. This dish can be seen in a tapas bar, or on a menu as a starter, and is traditionally served in Spanish homes as a side dish.

20 g (1 oz) butter
1 brown onion, chopped
175 g (6 oz) jamón or prosciutto, roughly chopped
2 garlic cloves, crushed

500 g (1 lb 2 oz) broad (fava) beans, fresh or frozen
125 ml (4 fl oz/½ cup) dry white wine
185 ml (6 fl oz/¾ cup) chicken stock

Melt the butter in a large saucepan and add the onion, jamón and crushed garlic. Cook over medium heat for 5 minutes, stirring often, until the onion softens.

Add the broad beans and wine and cook over high heat until the liquid is reduced by half. Add the stock, reduce the heat to low–medium, cover and cook for 10 minutes. Uncover and simmer for another 10 minutes or until the broad beans are tender and most of the liquid has evaporated. Serve hot as a tapas dish with crusty bread, or as a side dish.

SERVES 4

Empanadas de Atún

Tuna Empanadas

Originally from Galicia, the empanada is Spain's version of the pie. It would have been a satisfying snack for the hardy Galicians, who for centuries have been farmers and fishermen. Today, it comes with a variety of fillings, but the tuna version is a favourite.

400 g (14 oz/3¼ cups) plain (all-purpose) flour, plus extra for rolling
75 g (3 oz) butter, softened
2 eggs
60 ml (2 fl oz/¼ cup) fine sherry
1 egg, extra, lightly beaten

FILLING
1 tablespoon olive oil
1 small brown onion, finely diced
2 teaspoons tomato paste (concentrated purée)
125 g (5 oz/½ cup) tinned chopped tomatoes
85 g (3 oz) tinned tuna, drained
1½ tablespoons chopped roasted red capsicum (pepper), (see page 246)
2 tablespoons chopped flat-leaf (Italian) parsley

Sift the flour and 1 teaspoon of salt into a large bowl. Rub the butter into the flour until the mixture resembles fine breadcrumbs. Add the combined eggs and sherry to the bowl, cutting the liquid in with a flat-bladed knife until the mixture clumps and forms a dough. Turn onto a lightly floured surface and gather the dough together into a smooth ball (do not knead or you will have tough pastry). Cover with plastic wrap and refrigerate for 30 minutes.

To make the filling, heat the olive oil in a frying pan over medium heat and cook the onion for about 5 minutes, or until softened and translucent. Add the tomato paste and chopped tomato and cook for 10 minutes, or until pulpy. Add the tuna, roasted capsicum and parsley and season well.

Preheat the oven to 190°C (375°F/Gas 5). Dust a work surface with the extra flour. Roll out half the pastry to a thickness of 2 mm (¹/₁₆ in). Using a 10 cm (4 in) cutter, cut into 12 rounds. Put a heaped tablespoon of filling on each round, fold over and brush the edges with water, then pinch to seal. Continue with the remaining rounds, then repeat with the remaining dough and filling to make 24 empanadas.

Transfer to a lightly oiled baking tray and brush each empanada with the extra beaten egg. Bake for about 30 minutes, or until golden. Serve warm or cold.

MAKES 24

OLIVES

❁❁❁❁❁❁❁❁❁❁❁❁❁❁❁❁❁❁❁❁❁❁❁❁❁❁❁

To an outsider, it is remarkable the extent to which Spanish life and cuisine are lubricated by the fruit of the olive tree. Every bar or café on the peninsula will have a small dish of the fruits of that tree, and every kitchen at least one bottle of green cold oil.

Having arrived in Spain around 1000 BC with the Phoenicians and the Greeks, the olive tree was further cultivated by the Romans, and then by the Moors, who occupied Spain from 700 to 1492. The Spanish words for the olive (aceituna) and olive oil (aceite) come from the Arabic word, al-zait, meaning 'olive juice'.

Olives grow south of a line drawn across Spain, from Gerona in the east to the Portuguese border in the west. The further south you travel, the more the landscape is carpeted with olive trees. Grown throughout Spain, the majority of olives used for olive oil production are from this region. Of the 262 varieties of olive grown in Spain, only about 24 are used to produce olive oil.

Producing between 600,000 and 900,000 tonnes of olive oil per year, out of an annual global total of 2.6 million tonnes, olive oil is big business in Spain. While much of the oil is sent around the world and mixed with other blends, the Spanish have begun to bottle and label this distinctly Spanish product as their own. The 'denominación de origen' initiative, a regulatory classification system, has also encouraged this. The label used for each region guarantees the authenticity of the product as one of the highest quality in Spain.

Olive oil is widely enjoyed, with its medical and dietary benefits encouraging further use. Producing a range of flavours, a good-quality olive oil will have the lowest degree of acidity, with the most intense, full flavour. Other types of oil are fruity and fresh, with hints of almond and apple.

Some Spanish olive oil is still made according to the traditional method. The fruit, once picked and washed, is crushed and loaded onto mats made of esparta grass. The olive paste is then pressed to release a mixture of oil and water. Allowed to rest in stainless-steel vats, the oil and water separate. The oil is then bottled, the top sealed with wax. Olive oil, unlike most wines, is best enjoyed soon after bottling.

The modern method of olive oil production, using centrifugal machines, has brought quite a few benefits to the olive oil industry, improving the speed with which the olives can be processed after harvesting. This reduces the chance of fermentation and improves the quality of the final product. Organic olive oil is becoming more prevalent, but with strict guidelines governing how it is produced.

The fruit of the tree is also eaten, the best cured in brine for between one and six months. And around Christmas, the cracked green olives appear, eagerly awaited by many. These are the first picked of the season, cracked with a hammer, then brine cured, often with fresh fennel stalks. Which takes us back to the Phoenicians – today's Lebanese – who cure olives in the same way, even today.

Tortillitas de Gambas

Prawn Fritters

These fritters are made either with chopped prawns (shrimp) – gambas – or with the little camarones found in Andalucía. They are a simple and sensational addition to any table of tapas, but they can also be served with aperitifs before dinner.

60 g (2 oz/½ cup) plain (all-purpose) flour, sifted
55 g (2 oz/½ cup) besan (chickpea flour), sifted
1 teaspoon sweet paprika (pimentón)
4 large eggs, lightly beaten
4 spring onions (scallions), finely chopped

1 large handful flat-leaf (Italian) parsley, finely chopped
500 g (1 lb 2 oz) peeled and finely chopped raw prawns (shrimp), about 800 g (1 lb 12 oz) unpeeled
125 ml (4 fl oz/½ cup) olive oil
lemon wedges, to serve

Combine the flours in a bowl with the paprika and make a well in the centre. Pour in the egg and mix in gradually, then stir in 60 ml (2 fl oz/¼ cup) water to make a smooth batter. Add the spring onion, parsley and prawns and season well. Rest the batter for at least 30 minutes.

Heat the olive oil in a deep-sided frying pan over low–medium heat. Working in batches, spoon in

½ tablespoons of batter per fritter and flatten into a thin pancake. Cook for 2–3 minutes each side, or until golden and cooked through. Remove from the pan and drain on paper towel. Repeat with the remaining batter to make 24 fritters. Season well and serve with lemon wedges.

MAKES 24

Right: Spoon a small amount of the mixture into the hot oil for each fritter.

Far right: Cook the fritters until golden on each side.

CHORIZO EN SIDRA

Chorizo in Cider

Grapevines do not grow in the mountainous north, so cider is the beverage of choice in Asturias, Galicia and Basque country where the climate is ideal for growing apples. The fruity acidity of cider teams wonderfully with spicy chorizo in this dish.

3 teaspoons olive oil
1 small brown onion, finely chopped
1½ teaspoons sweet paprika (pimentón)
125 ml (4 fl oz/½ cup) sidra (alcoholic apple cider)
60 ml (2 fl oz/¼ cup) chicken stock

1 bay leaf
2 chorizo, approximately 300 g (11 oz) in total, sliced diagonally
2 teaspoons sherry vinegar, or to taste
2 teaspoons chopped flat-leaf (Italian) parsley

Heat the olive oil in a saucepan over low heat, add the onion and cook for 5 minutes, or until soft, stirring occasionally. Add the paprika and cook for 1 minute.

Increase the heat to medium, add the cider, stock and bay leaf to the pan and bring to the boil.

Reduce the heat and simmer for 5 minutes. Add the chorizo and simmer for 5 minutes, or until the sauce has reduced slightly. Stir in the sherry vinegar and parsley. Season to taste. Serve hot.

SERVES 4

CROQUETAS

Croquettes

These little deep-fried snacks are universally loved for their sublime symphony of crunchy outside and creamy inside. The inside, if perfect, will explode in the mouth with rich flavour – in the case of this particular recipe, of jamón.

90 g (3 oz) butter
1 small brown onion, finely chopped
115 g (4 oz) open cap mushrooms, finely chopped
125 g (5 oz/1 cup) plain (all-purpose) flour
250 ml (9 fl oz/1 cup) milk
185 ml (6 fl oz/³⁄₄ cup) chicken stock

115 g (4 oz) jamón or prosciutto, finely chopped
60 g (2 oz/¹⁄₂ cup) plain (all-purpose) flour, extra
2 eggs, lightly beaten
50 g (2 oz/¹⁄₂ cup) dry breadcrumbs
olive oil, for deep-frying

Melt the butter in a saucepan over low heat, add the onion and cook for 5 minutes, or until translucent. Add the mushrooms and cook over low heat, stirring occasionally, for 5 minutes. Add the flour and stir over low–medium heat for 1 minute, or until the mixture is dry and crumbly and begins to change colour. Remove from the heat and gradually add the milk, stirring until smooth. Stir in the stock and return to the heat, stirring until the mixture boils and thickens. Stir in the jamón and some black pepper, then transfer the mixture to a bowl to cool for about 2 hours.

Roll heaped tablespoons of the mixture into croquette shapes about 6 cm (2¹⁄₂ in) long. Put

the extra flour, beaten egg and breadcrumbs in three separate shallow bowls. Toss the croquettes in the flour, dip in the egg, allowing the excess to drain away, then roll in the breadcrumbs. Put on a baking tray and refrigerate for about 30 minutes.

Fill a deep, heavy-based saucepan one-third full of oil. Heat the oil to 170°C (325°F), or until a cube of bread dropped into the oil browns in 20 seconds. Add the croquettes in batches and deep-fry for 3 minutes, turning, until brown. Drain well on paper towel. Sprinkle with salt before serving hot.

MAKES 24

Right: Pour in the chicken stock and stir until the mixture boils and thickens.

Far right: Once formed, refrigerate the croquettes to help set the flour, egg and breadcrumb coating before frying.

Aceitunas Picantes
Chilli Olives

In every bar in Spain you will find bowls of olives, the best cured in brine for up to six months. This dish melds olives from the Old World, chillies from the New and spices from the East, highlighting the convergence of influences on Spanish food.

3 garlic cloves, thinly sliced
2 tablespoons vinegar or lemon juice
500 g (1 lb 2 oz) cured (wrinkled) black olives
1 handful chopped flat-leaf (Italian) parsley

1 tablespoon chilli flakes
3 teaspoons crushed coriander seeds
2 teaspoons crushed cumin seeds
500 ml (17 fl oz/2 cups) olive oil

Soak the garlic slices in the vinegar or lemon juice for 24 hours. Drain and mix in a bowl with the olives, parsley, chilli flakes, coriander and cumin.

Sterilize a 1 litre (35 fl oz/4 cup) wide-necked jar by rinsing with boiling water, then drying in a warm oven. Don't dry it with a tea towel (dish towel).

Spoon the olive mixture into the jar and pour in the olive oil. Seal and marinate in the refrigerator for 1–2 weeks before serving at room temperature. The marinated olives will keep for a further month in the refrigerator.

FILLS A 1 LITRE (35 FL OZ/4 CUP) JAR

Patatas Allioli
Fried Potatoes with Garlic Mayonnaise

Another simple and delicious dish that can be found in tapas bars throughout Spain. Who was it who first had the brilliant idea of putting garlic in mayonnaise? Ask any Spaniard and they will tell you that it was the Catalans, of course!

750 g (1 lb 10 oz) all-purpose potatoes, peeled
60 ml (2 fl oz/¼ cup) olive oil

allioli (see page 249)

Preheat the oven to 200°C (400°F/Gas 6). Cut the potatoes into 4 cm (1½ in) cubes and put on a baking tray with the olive oil. Mix to coat and season well. Cook in the oven for 45 minutes, or until golden. Shake the baking tray occasionally so the potatoes bake evenly on all sides.

Season the potatoes and serve with the allioli dolloped over the top or served on the side for dipping. Any leftover allioli can be kept in an airtight container in the refrigerator for 2–3 days.

SERVES 4–6

BANDERILLAS (PINCHOS)

Tuna Skewers

Tapas on skewers – banderillas in the south, pinchos in the north – are your chance to assemble, on the little stick, a clever collection of complementary flavours, as exemplified here with tuna, caper berries and green olives.

250 g (9 oz) raw tuna
1 lemon
1 tablespoon lemon juice

1 tablespoon extra virgin olive oil
16 caper berries
8 green olives, stuffed with anchovies

Soak eight wooden skewers in cold water for 1 hour to prevent them burning during cooking. Cut the tuna into 24 even-sized cubes. Remove the zest from the lemon, avoiding the bitter white pith, and cut the zest into thin strips.

Combine the tuna, lemon zest, lemon juice and olive oil in a bowl.

Thread three pieces of tuna, two caper berries and one green olive onto each skewer, alternating each ingredient. Put in a non-metallic dish and pour the marinade over them. Cook under a hot grill (broiler), turning to cook each side, for 4 minutes, or until done to your liking.

PICTURE ON PAGE 44

MAKES 8

Tuna Skewers (recipe on page 43)

POLLO EN SALSA DE AJO
Chicken in Garlic Sauce

A fine example of a modern recipe that takes typical and traditional ingredients – in this case, lots of garlic and sherry – and combines them in a way that is so impressive the dish will soon enter your repertoire of everyday meals.

1 kg (2 lb 4 oz) boneless, skinless chicken thighs
1 tablespoon sweet paprika (pimentón)
2 tablespoons olive oil
8 garlic cloves, unpeeled

60 ml (2 fl oz/¼ cup) fino sherry
125 ml (4 fl oz/½ cup) chicken stock
1 bay leaf
2 tablespoons chopped flat-leaf (Italian) parsley

Trim any excess fat from the chicken and cut the thighs into thirds. Combine the paprika with some salt and pepper in a bowl, add the chicken and toss to coat.

Heat half the oil in a large frying pan over high heat and cook the garlic cloves for 1–2 minutes, or until brown. Remove from the pan. Cook the chicken in batches for 5 minutes, or until brown all over. Return all the chicken to the pan, add the sherry, boil for 30 seconds, then add the stock and bay leaf. Reduce the heat and simmer, covered, over low heat for 10 minutes.

Meanwhile, squeeze the garlic pulp from the skins and pound with the parsley into a paste using a mortar and pestle or a small bowl and the back of a spoon. Stir into the chicken, then cover and cook for 10 minutes, or until tender. Serve hot.

SERVES 6

Use a mortar and pestle to pound the garlic pulp and the parsley to form a paste.

Pimientos Escabechados

Marinated Capsicums

Brought back from the New World by Columbus – like so much Spanish food – no vegetable has entered the Spanish repertoire more completely than the pimiento, the capsicum or bell pepper, in all its shapes and colours.

3 red capsicums (peppers), roasted (see page 246)
3 thyme sprigs
1 garlic clove, thinly sliced
2 teaspoons roughly chopped flat-leaf (Italian) parsley
1 bay leaf

1 spring onion (scallion), sliced
1 teaspoon sweet paprika (pimentón)
60 ml (2 fl oz/¼ cup) extra virgin olive oil
2 tablespoons red wine vinegar

Slice the capsicums thinly, then place in a bowl with the thyme, garlic, parsley, bay leaf and spring onion. Mix well.

Whisk together the paprika, olive oil and vinegar and season with salt and pepper. Pour over the capsicum mixture and toss to combine. Cover and refrigerate for at least 3 hours, or preferably overnight, stirring once or twice during this period. Remove from the refrigerator about 30 minutes before serving.

SERVES 6

Charring the capsicums enables easy peeling and tenderizes the sweet flesh.

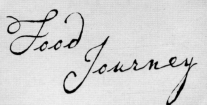

Food Journey

SHERRY

∞∞∞∞∞∞∞∞∞∞∞∞∞∞∞∞∞∞∞∞∞∞∞∞∞∞∞∞∞∞∞∞∞

*Only three towns in the province of
Andalucía produce one of the world's
most mysterious, misunderstood and
exquisite wines, sherry: Jerez de la
Frontera, Puerto de Santa Maria and
Sanlucar de Barrameda. If it does not
come from what is called the sherry
triangle, it is not sherry.*

The story of sherry – or jerez (pronounced
hereth) – begins with the Phoenicians, passes
through Elizabethan England where it was highly
prized as sherry sack, and curves back into Spain,
where it is produced as it always has been, and
drunk, especially in the south, as a wine would
be, as an accompaniment to food.

Sherry is often sadly misunderstood, thought of
as sickly sweet and cloying. The variety of sherry
though is overwhelming: fino, drunk chilled and
as fresh as possible; amontillado, beginning life as
a fino, but reclassified when it is fortified; oloroso,
darker as it ages and occasionally blended with
the 'sweeter' sherries; and finally, Pedro Ximénez,

the rich and luscious Christmas pudding of sherry, which is divine served with chocolate.

Sherry is the result of a fortuitous meeting of fruit, climate and airborne ferments, the flor, a yeast that settles on the fermented must. Its production is quite complex, involving ageing a fairly ordinary dry white wine using the solera system: a series of wine-filled casks, graded by age, blended from small amounts of the oldest, to larger amounts of the youngest.

Mysteriously, sherry is also exposed to the one element that is the enemy of all other wines: air. Oxidization is used to enrich flavour and colour. Finally, all sherry is fortified with brandy. The other mystery is the genesis of the process. At what point did the winemakers of the triangle hit upon the very complex method of turning a boring white wine into one of the wine wonders of the world?

Revuelto de Espárragos

Scrambled Eggs with Asparagus

Creamy scrambled eggs as a starter? Why not? That's what the Spanish call a revuelto: scrambled eggs with fresh seasonal ingredients like prawns, mushrooms, garlic shoots, baby artichokes and, in the case of this delicious recipe, asparagus.

2 garlic cloves, chopped
1 thick slice bread, crusts removed
60 ml (2 fl oz/¼ cup) olive oil
175 g (6 oz/1 bunch) asparagus, cut into
    2 cm (¾ in) lengths

1 teaspoon sweet paprika (pimentón)
2 tablespoons white wine vinegar
6 eggs, beaten

Put the garlic and bread in a food processor or mortar and pestle and grind to a loose paste, adding a little water (1–2 tablespoons).

Heat the oil in a frying pan over medium heat and sauté the asparagus for 2 minutes, or until just starting to become tender. Add the garlic paste, paprika, vinegar and a pinch of salt, and stir to combine. Cover and cook over medium heat for 2–3 minutes, or until the asparagus is tender.

Pour in the beaten eggs and gently stir for a few minutes. Remove the mixture from the heat just before it is fully cooked (the perfect revuelto is creamy in consistency), then season to taste and serve immediately.

SERVES 4

Far left: Combine the asparagus pieces and the garlic paste and cook until tender.

Left: Stir in the eggs and cook until creamy.

GARBANZOS CON CHORIZO
Chickpeas with Chorizo

This combination of two emblematic ingredients of Spanish cooking provides a simple but satisfying tapas dish. Chorizo, a sometimes fiery sausage of pork and pimentón, is eaten right across Spain, from San Sebastián to Sevilla, Barcelona to Badajoz.

165 g (6 oz/¾ cup) dried chickpeas
1 bay leaf
4 cloves
1 cinnamon stick
750 ml (26 fl oz/3 cups) chicken stock
2 tablespoons olive oil

1 brown onion, finely chopped
1 garlic clove, crushed
pinch of dried thyme
375 g (13 oz) chorizo, chopped (slightly larger
   than the chickpeas)
1 tablespoon chopped flat-leaf (Italian) parsley

Put the chickpeas in a large bowl, cover with water and soak overnight. Drain well, then combine in a large saucepan with the bay leaf, cloves, cinnamon stick and stock. Cover completely with water, then bring to the boil. Reduce the heat and simmer for 1 hour, or until the chickpeas are tender. If they need longer, add a little more water and continue cooking. There should be just a little liquid left in the saucepan. Drain and remove the bay leaf, cloves and cinnamon stick.

Heat the oil in a large frying pan, add the onion and cook over medium heat for 3 minutes, or until translucent. Add the garlic and thyme and cook, stirring, for 1 minute. Increase the heat to medium–high, add the chorizo and cook for 3 minutes.

Add the chickpeas to the frying pan, mix well, then stir over medium heat for about 4 minutes or until they are heated through. Remove from the heat and mix in the parsley. Taste before seasoning with salt and freshly ground black pepper. This dish is equally delicious served hot or at room temperature.

SERVES 6

Mejillones Rellenos

Stuffed Mussels

Mussels are cheaper and more versatile than their mollusc relation, the oyster, and as such, are more common. They lend themselves to a great number of preparations, including this texturally appealing dish, infused with the delicious flavour of garlic.

18 black mussels
2 teaspoons olive oil
2 spring onions (scallions), finely chopped
1 garlic clove, crushed
1 tablespoon tomato paste (concentrated purée)
2 teaspoons lemon juice
1 large handful flat-leaf (Italian) parsley, chopped
75 g (3 oz/¾ cup) dry breadcrumbs
2 eggs, beaten
olive oil, for deep-frying

WHITE SAUCE
20 g (¾ oz) butter
1½ tablespoons plain (all-purpose) flour
2 tablespoons milk

Scrub the mussels and remove the hairy beards. Discard any open mussels or those that don't close when tapped on the bench.

Bring 250 ml (9 fl oz/1 cup) water to the boil in a saucepan, add the mussels, then cover and cook for 3–4 minutes, shaking the pan occasionally, until the mussels have just opened. Remove them as soon as they open or they will be tough. Strain the cooking liquid into a pitcher until you have 80 ml (3 fl oz/⅓ cup). Discard any unopened mussels. Remove the other mussels from their shells and discard one half shell from each. Finely chop the mussel meat.

Heat the oil in a frying pan, add the spring onion and cook for 1 minute. Add the garlic and cook for 1 minute. Stir in the mussel meat, tomato paste, lemon juice, 2 tablespoons of the parsley and season with salt and pepper. Set aside to cool.

To make the white sauce, melt the butter in a saucepan over low heat. Stir in the flour and cook for 1 minute, or until pale and foaming. Remove

from the heat and gradually whisk in the reserved mussel liquid, the milk and some pepper. Return to the heat and cook, stirring, for 1 minute, or until the sauce boils and thickens. Reduce the heat and simmer for 2 minutes, or until quite thick. Cool.

Spoon the mussel mixture into the shells. Top each generously with the thick white sauce and smooth the surface, to form a mound.

Combine the breadcrumbs and the remaining parsley. Dip the mussels in the egg, then press in the crumbs to cover the top. Fill a deep, heavy-based saucepan one-third full of oil and heat to 180°C (350°F), or until a cube of bread browns in 15 seconds. Cook the mussels in batches for 10–15 seconds, or until lightly browned. Remove with a slotted spoon and drain well. Serve hot.

MAKES 18

CHAMPIÑONES AL AJILLO

Garlic Mushrooms

Garlic, in Spain, is not used with subtlety, but with gusto and abandon, as in this favoured tapas dish. This tasty but simple dish of garlic and mushrooms appears on menus at cafés and bars right across the Iberian Peninsula.

6 garlic cloves
1½ tablespoons lemon juice
650 g (1 lb 7 oz) mushrooms (such as button, Swiss brown or pine), sliced

60 ml (2 fl oz/¼ cup) olive oil
½ small red chilli, seeded and finely chopped
2 teaspoons chopped flat-leaf (Italian) parsley

Crush four of the garlic cloves and thinly slice the rest. Sprinkle the lemon juice all over the sliced mushrooms.

Heat the oil in a large frying pan and add the crushed garlic and chopped chilli. Stir over medium–high heat for 10 seconds, then add the mushrooms. Season and cook, stirring often, for 8–10 minutes or until the mushrooms are tender. Stir in the sliced garlic and chopped parsley and cook for another minute. Serve hot.

PICTURE ON OPPOSITE PAGE

SERVES 4

PAN CON TOMATE

Toast with Tomato

Also known as pan a la Catalana, this humble, straightforward dish is a favourite in tapas bars throughout Spain. Serve it with the freshest, ripest tomatoes you can find for a truly luscious experience.

1 crusty bread stick
6 garlic cloves, halved

3 tomatoes, halved
extra virgin olive oil, for drizzling

Slice the bread stick diagonally and toast the slices very lightly. Rub them on one side with a cut garlic clove, then with half a tomato, squeezing the juice onto the bread. Season with a little salt and drizzle with extra virgin olive oil.

SERVES 6

Ensaladilla Russa

Russian Salad

The mystery of the Russian salad is one people like to speculate about, as they enjoy it with a cold beer. Why is a potato and artichoke salad hailing from Russia to be found in every tapas bar in Spain? No matter – one bite and you won't care where it came from!

MAYONNAISE
2 egg yolks
1 teaspoon dijon mustard
125 ml (4 fl oz/½ cup) extra virgin olive oil (see note)
2 tablespoons lemon juice
2 small garlic cloves, crushed

3 bottled artichoke hearts
3 all-purpose potatoes, such as desiree, unpeeled
100 g (4 oz) baby green beans, trimmed and cut into 1 cm (½ in) lengths

1 large carrot, cut into 1 cm (½ in) dice
125 g (5 oz) fresh peas
30 g (1 oz) cornichons, chopped
2 tablespoons baby capers, rinsed and drained
4 anchovy fillets, finely chopped
10 black olives, each cut into 3 slices
whole black olives, extra, to garnish

To make the mayonnaise, use electric beaters to beat the egg yolks with the mustard and ¼ teaspoon salt until creamy. Gradually add the oil in a fine stream, beating constantly until all the oil has been added. Add the lemon juice, garlic and 1 teaspoon boiling water and beat for 1 minute, or until well combined. Season to taste.

Cut each artichoke into quarters. Rinse the potatoes, cover with salted cold water and bring to a gentle simmer. Cook for 15–20 minutes, or until tender when pierced with a knife. Drain and allow to cool slightly. Peel and set aside. When the potatoes are completely cool, cut them into 1 cm (½ in) dice.

Blanch the beans in salted boiling water until tender but still firm to the bite. Refresh in cold water, then drain thoroughly. Repeat with the carrot and peas.

Set aside a small quantity of each vegetable, including the cornichons, for the garnish and season to taste. Put the remainder in a bowl with the capers, anchovies and sliced olives. Add the mayonnaise, toss to combine and season. Arrange on a serving dish and garnish with the reserved vegetables and the whole olives.

NOTE: Use a low-acid or mild-flavoured olive oil to prevent any bitterness.

SERVES 4–6

PATATAS BRAVAS
Potatoes in Spicy Tomato Sauce

A dish rarely seen outside the tapas bar, it can, like the simple Spanish tortilla, reveal the quality of the rest of the offerings at a bar. The signs of a good patatas bravas are potatoes that are firm to the mouth but not starchy, and a sauce that is deeply spicy.

1 kg (2 lb 4 oz) all-purpose potatoes, such as desiree
oil, for deep-frying
2 tablespoons olive oil
¼ red onion, finely chopped
2 garlic cloves, crushed
3 teaspoons sweet paprika (pimentón)

¼ teaspoon cayenne pepper
500 g (1 lb 2 oz) ripe roma (plum) tomatoes, peeled,
   seeded and chopped (see page 246)
1 bay leaf
1 teaspoon white sugar

Peel the potatoes, then cut into 2 cm (¾ in) cubes. Rinse, then drain well and pat completely dry. Fill a deep-fryer or large heavy-based saucepan one-third full of oil and heat to 180°C (350°F), or until a cube of bread dropped into the oil browns in 15 seconds. Cook the potato in batches for 5 minutes, or until golden. Drain well on paper towel. Do not discard the oil.

Heat the oil in a saucepan over medium heat and cook the onion for 5 minutes, or until softened. Add the garlic, paprika and cayenne pepper and cook for 1–2 minutes, or until fragrant.

Add the tomato, bay leaf, sugar and 80 ml (3 fl oz/ ⅓ cup) water and cook, stirring occasionally, for

20 minutes, or until thick and pulpy. Cool slightly and remove the bay leaf. Blend in a food processor until smooth, adding a little water if necessary. Before serving, return the sauce to the saucepan and simmer over low heat for 2 minutes, or until heated through. Season well.

Reheat the oil to 180°C (350°F) and cook the potato again, in batches, for 2 minutes, or until very crisp and golden. Drain on paper towel. This second frying makes the potato extra crispy and stops the sauce soaking in immediately. Put on a platter and cover with sauce. Serve immediately.

SERVES 6

A double-frying of the cubes of potato gives them an especially crunchy result.

Buñuelos de Bacalao
Salt Cod Fritters

These fritters are a classic Catalan tapas dish and are a testament to the enduring appeal of bacalao (salt cod), first brought to Spain by Basque fishermen. This dish is so popular that it is even served as an appetizer in some of the better restaurants.

500 g (1 lb 2 oz) bacalao (salt cod)
1 large (200 g/7 oz) all-purpose potato, such as desiree, unpeeled
2 tablespoons milk
60 ml (2 fl oz/¼ cup) olive oil
1 small white onion, finely chopped

2 garlic cloves, crushed
30 g (1 oz/¼ cup) self-raising flour
2 eggs, separated
1 tablespoon chopped flat-leaf (Italian) parsley
olive oil, extra, for deep-frying

Soak the bacalao in plenty of cold water in the fridge for about 20 hours, changing the water four or five times to remove excess saltiness.

Cook the potato in a saucepan of boiling water for 20 minutes, or until soft. When cool, peel and mash the potato with the milk and 2 tablespoons of the olive oil.

Drain the bacalao, cut into large pieces and put in a saucepan. Cover with water, bring to the boil over high heat, then reduce the heat to medium and cook for 10 minutes, or until the fish is soft and there is a froth on the surface. Drain. When cool enough to handle, remove the skin and any bones, then mash the flesh with a fork until flaky.

Heat the remaining oil in a small frying pan and cook the onion over medium heat for 5 minutes, or until softened and starting to brown. Add the garlic and cook for 1 minute. Remove from the heat.

Combine the potato, bacalao, onion and garlic, flour, egg yolks and parsley in a bowl and season. Whisk the egg whites until stiff, then fold into the mixture. Fill a deep-fryer or large heavy-based saucepan one-third full of olive oil and heat to 190°C (375°F), or until a cube of bread dropped into the oil browns in 10 seconds. Drop heaped tablespoons of the mixture into the oil and cook, turning once, for 2–3 minutes, or until puffed and golden. Drain well and serve immediately.

MAKES ABOUT 36

Right: Flake the bacalao well with a fork so it incorporates easily with the other ingredients.

Far right: Deep-fry the fritters in the hot oil until they are puffed and golden brown.

ALBÓNDIGAS
Meatballs

While you'll find meatballs of some incarnation all over the world, none is as flavoursome as the albóndiga. Originally Moorish, these meatballs are recognizable through the rich sauce, golden-fried appearance and generous use of spices.

175 g (6 oz) minced (ground) pork
175 g (6 oz) minced (ground) veal
3 garlic cloves, crushed
35 g (1 oz/⅓ cup) dry breadcrumbs
1 teaspoon ground coriander
1 teaspoon ground nutmeg
1 teaspoon ground cumin
pinch of ground cinnamon
1 egg
2 tablespoons olive oil

SPICY TOMATO SAUCE
1 tablespoon olive oil
1 brown onion, chopped
2 garlic cloves, crushed
125 ml (4 fl oz/½ cup) dry white wine
400 g (14 oz) tinned chopped tomatoes
1 tablespoon tomato paste (concentrated purée)
125 ml (4 fl oz/½ cup) chicken stock
½ teaspoon cayenne pepper
80 g (3 oz/½ cup) frozen peas

Combine the pork, veal, garlic, breadcrumbs, spices, egg and season with salt and pepper in a bowl. Mix by hand until the mixture is smooth and leaves the side of the bowl. Refrigerate, covered, for 30 minutes.

Roll tablespoons of the mixture into balls. Heat 1 tablespoon of olive oil in a frying pan and toss half the meatballs over medium–high heat for 2–3 minutes, or until browned. Drain on paper towel. Add the remaining oil and brown the rest of the meatballs. Drain on paper towel.

To make the sauce, heat the oil in a frying pan over medium heat and cook the onion, stirring occasionally, for 3 minutes, or until translucent. Add the garlic and cook for 1 minute. Increase the heat to high, add the white wine and boil for 1 minute. Add the chopped tomatoes, tomato paste and stock and simmer for 10 minutes. Stir in the cayenne pepper, peas and meatballs and simmer for 5–10 minutes, or until the sauce is thick. Serve hot.

SERVES 6

Right: Combine the minced pork and veal with the remaining ingredients and mix thoroughly.

Far right: Brown the meatballs well to enhance the flavours.

MIGAS CON HUEVOS

Fried Breadcrumbs with Eggs

Breadcrumbs are an ingredient of 'la cocina pobre' – the cuisine of the poor – as was bacalao. And breadcrumbs, like bacalao, have become chic – or, as the Spanish would say, 'la moda'. Here they team perfectly with eggs.

4 thick slices white bread, crusts removed
2 tablespoons extra virgin olive oil
125 ml (4 fl oz/½ cup), mild olive oil
1 red onion, cut into 2 cm (¾ in) cubes
2 garlic cloves, crushed
2 red capsicums (peppers), cut into 2 cm (¾ in) squares

100 g (4 oz) thinly sliced jamón, cut into fine strips
2 chorizo, cut into 2 cm (¾ in) cubes
½ teaspoon smoked Spanish paprika
4 eggs
2 tablespoons chopped flat-leaf (Italian) parsley

Cut or tear the bread into small pieces or large crumbs. Heat the extra virgin olive oil in a large heavy-based frying pan over medium heat. Add the bread pieces and toss to coat in the oil, then stir continuously for 3–4 minutes or until lightly golden. Remove and drain on paper towel. Season with salt and pepper and allow to cool.

Heat 2 tablespoons of the mild olive oil in the same pan used for the bread over medium heat. Add the onion, garlic and red capsicum and stir until softened, about 10 minutes. Add the jamón, chorizo and paprika and continue to cook on medium heat until lightly browned, another 10 minutes. Sprinkle with half the bread pieces

and stir through. Remove from the heat and keep warm in a low oven while cooking the eggs.

Put the remaining oil in a clean frying pan over medium heat. When hot, quickly crack four eggs into the oil. Using a metal spoon, scoop hot oil from the base of the pan over the eggs so that they become crisp around the edges while the yolks remain soft. Remove from the oil and drain on paper towel.

To serve, divide the breadcrumb mixture among four serving dishes; top each with a fried egg and sprinkle with parsley.

SERVES 4

Chapter 2

SEAFOOD

With a coastline stretching from France to Africa, and being lapped
by the Mediterranean, the Atlantic and the Cantabrian Sea,
it's little wonder that seafood is a mainstay in Spain.

ALMEJAS AL VINO BLANCO
Clams in White Wine

What could be simpler and more delicious than fresh clams steamed open in white wine and garlic, the flavours mingling with the clams' own juices of the sea? Try this modern version of almejas a la marinera from Cantabria, on the northern coast.

1 kg (2 lb 4 oz) clams (vongole)
2 tablespoons olive oil
1 small onion, finely chopped
2 garlic cloves, crushed
2 large ripe tomatoes, peeled, seeded and chopped
  (see page 246)

1 tablespoon chopped flat-leaf (Italian) parsley
pinch of ground nutmeg
80 ml (3 fl oz/⅓ cup) dry white wine

Soak the clams in salted water for 2 hours to release any grit. Rinse under running water and discard any open clams.

Heat the oil in a large flameproof casserole dish and cook the onion over low heat for 8 minutes, or until softened. Add the garlic and chopped tomato and cook for 5 minutes. Stir in the parsley and ground nutmeg and season with salt and pepper. Add 80 ml (3 fl oz/⅓ cup) of water.

Add the clams and cook, covered, over low heat for 5–8 minutes or until they open (discard any that do not open). Add the wine and cook for 3–4 minutes, or until the sauce thickens, gently moving the dish back and forth a few times, rather than stirring, so that the clams stay in the shells. Serve immediately, with bread.

SERVES 4

GAMBAS CON SALSA ROMESCO
Prawns with Romesco Sauce

This classic Catalan sauce is from the town of Tarragona, best made with the romesco or nyora capsicum (pepper), though ancho chillies or any dried capsicum will also work well. Romesco sauce is famed as the basis of Catalan seafood stew.

30 raw large prawns (shrimp)
1 tablespoon olive oil

ROMESCO SAUCE
4 garlic cloves, unpeeled
1 roma (plum) tomato, halved and seeded

2 long red chillies
2 tablespoons whole blanched almonds
2 tablespoons hazelnuts
60 g (2 oz) sun-dried capsicums (peppers) in oil
1 tablespoon olive oil
1 tablespoon red wine vinegar

Peel the prawns, leaving the tails intact. Cut down the back and gently pull out the dark vein, starting at the head end. Mix the prawns with ¼ teaspoon salt and refrigerate for 30 minutes.

To make the romesco sauce, preheat the oven to 200°C (400°F/Gas 6). Wrap the garlic cloves in foil, put on a baking tray with the tomato and chillies and bake for about 12 minutes. Spread the almonds and hazelnuts on the tray and bake for another 3–5 minutes. Leave to cool for 15 minutes. Peel the skin off the tomato.

Transfer the almonds and hazelnuts to a small blender or food processor and blend until finely ground. Squeeze the garlic, and the tomato flesh, into the blender, discarding the skins. Split the chillies and remove the seeds. Scrape the flesh into the blender, discarding the skins. Pat the capsicums dry with paper towel, then chop them and add to the blender with the oil, vinegar, some salt and 2 tablespoons water. Blend until smooth, adding more water, if necessary, to form a soft dipping consistency. Set aside for 30 minutes.

Heat the olive oil in a frying pan over high heat and cook the prawns for 5 minutes, or until curled up and slightly pink. Serve with the sauce.

SERVES 6–8

Right: Making a cut down the back of the prawn will assist in removing the dark vein.

Far right: Blend the sauce ingredients in a food processor until the sauce reaches a smooth dipping consistency.

MERLUZA EN SALSA VERDE

Hake in Green Sauce

A standard of Basque cuisine that today appears all over Spain, combining the country's most popular fish – merluza – with a light parsley sauce and fresh produce. Clams, monkfish or cod make excellent substitutes if hake is not available.

4 x 200 g (7 oz) hake steaks
seasoned plain (all-purpose) flour, for dusting
80 ml (3 fl oz/⅓ cup) olive oil
3 garlic cloves, chopped
2 green chillies, seeded and chopped
125 ml (4 fl oz/½ cup) white wine

170 ml (6 fl oz/⅔ cup) fish stock
1 large handful chopped flat-leaf (Italian) parsley
12 asparagus spears, lightly blanched and cut into
    4 cm (1½ in) lengths
60 g (2 oz/⅓ cup) cooked green peas

Dust the fish steaks with the seasoned flour, shaking off any excess.

Heat the olive oil in a large frying pan over medium heat and cook the garlic and chilli for 1 minute, or until the garlic just starts to colour. Remove the garlic and chilli with a slotted spoon. Increase the heat to high and cook the hake for about 1 minute each side or until lightly golden.

Remove from the pan. Add the wine, fish stock, half the parsley and the garlic and chilli mixture to the pan and simmer for a few minutes or until the sauce has thickened slightly.

Add the fish, asparagus, peas and remaining parsley to the pan. Simmer for a few minutes until the fish is cooked through. Serve immediately.

SERVES 4

Cooking the garlic until lightly golden brown gives it a slightly sweet and nutty flavour.

Pulpo en Salsa de Almendras

Octopus in Almond Garlic Sauce

This modern recipe, popular in coastal regions, combines classic ingredients from the Old World – octopus, garlic and almonds – with a classic ingredient from the New – capsicum (pepper). The result: a marriage of wonderful flavours and textures.

1 kg (2 lb 4 oz) baby octopus
½ small red capsicum (pepper), roasted (see page 246)
125 g (5 oz/1⅓ cups) flaked almonds
3 garlic cloves, crushed

80 ml (3 fl oz/⅓ cup) red wine vinegar
185 ml (6 fl oz/¾ cup) olive oil
2 tablespoons chopped flat-leaf (Italian) parsley

Using a small knife, carefully cut between the head and tentacles of the octopus and push the beak out and up through the centre of the tentacles using your fingers. Discard. Cut an arc around the eyes to remove them. To clean the head, carefully slit through one side and pull out or chop out the gut. Rinse the octopus under running water. Drop the octopus into a large saucepan of boiling water and simmer for 20–30 minutes, depending on the size, until tender. After 15 minutes, start pricking the octopus with a skewer to test for tenderness. When ready, remove from the heat and cool in the pan for 15 minutes.

To make the sauce, put the roasted red capsicum in a food processor with the almonds and garlic, and purée. With the motor running, gradually pour in the vinegar followed by the oil. Stir in 125 ml (4 fl oz/½ cup) boiling water and the parsley, and season to taste with salt and freshly ground black pepper.

To serve, cut the tentacles into pieces. Combine with the sauce. Serve warm, or chill and serve as a salad.

SERVES 4

Far left: Separate the octopus tentacles from the head just beneath the eyes.

Left: Carefully pull the gut from the head.

Caldo de Mariscos
Seafood Soup with Allioli

One of the many ways to celebrate the abundance and variety of seafood – inspired by the suquet of Catalonia and the tioro of the Basques. Simple and reliant only on the freshest mariscos – seafood – you can find. This hearty soup is sure to please.

1 tablespoon olive oil
1 carrot, finely diced
1 white onion, finely diced
1 leek, finely diced
3 garlic cloves, chopped
1 small red chilli, seeded and finely chopped
1 celery stalk, finely diced
2 large all-purpose potatoes, peeled and cut into
   2 cm (³/₄ in) dice
500 g (1 lb 2 oz) skinless firm white fish fillets, cut into
   2 cm (³/₄ in) cubes, reserving any bones and scraps
1 bay leaf

250 ml (9 fl oz/1 cup) white wine
30 ml (1 fl oz/1¹/₂ tablespoons) brandy
400 g (14 oz) tinned chopped tomatoes, drained
60 ml (2 fl oz/¹/₄ cup) tomato paste (concentrated purée)
12 black mussels, bearded and scrubbed
8 raw king prawns (shrimp), peeled and deveined,
   tails intact
2 tablespoons lemon juice
2 tablespoons chopped flat-leaf (Italian) parsley
fried bread, to serve (optional)
allioli (see page 249), to serve (optional)

Heat the olive oil in a large saucepan over medium heat. Add the carrot, onion, leek, garlic, red chilli and celery and cook for 5 minutes, or until the onion is translucent. Add the potato and 1.5 litres (52 fl oz/6 cups) of cold water. Bring to the boil, then reduce the heat and simmer for 8 minutes, or until the potatoes are half cooked. Stir in the fish bones and scraps and the bay leaf and simmer for 6–8 minutes, or until the potatoes are soft. Strain the liquid and reserve. Remove the bones and bay leaf, and purée the remaining potato and vegetable mixture with the reserved liquid.

In a separate saucepan, combine the white wine, brandy, chopped tomato and tomato paste and bring to the boil. Add the mussels and cook,

covered, for 3–5 minutes, or until opened. Remove from the pan, discarding any that remain closed.

Blend the mussel-cooking liquid with the potato purée. Transfer this mixture to a large saucepan and bring to the boil. Add the fish cubes and prawns, reduce the heat and simmer for 8 minutes, or until all the seafood is cooked.

Stir in the mussels and lemon juice and gently heat through. Season well and garnish with the parsley. Delicious served with fried bread and allioli.

PICTURE ON PAGE 84

SERVES 4–6

Seafood Soup with Allioli (recipe on page 83)

Salmón a la Sidra

Salmon in Cider

The icy rivers that run through the massive Picos de Europa (European Peaks) teem with salmon in the prime fishing season, from April to September. Fresh steaks were simply cooked with the local cider for a sensational regional dish.

12 clams (vongole)
2 tablespoons mild olive oil
4 salmon fillet pieces, 180–200 g (6–7 oz) each
3 tablespoons extra virgin olive oil
1 red onion, thinly sliced

350 ml (12 fl oz) sidra (alcoholic apple cider)
pinch of dried chilli powder
12 mussels, bearded and scrubbed
3 tablespoons finely chopped flat-leaf (Italian) parsley

Cover the clams in water and put in the fridge for 2 hours to remove any sand. Drain and rinse.

Preheat the oven to 180°C (350°F/Gas 4). Heat the mild olive oil in a heavy-based flameproof casserole dish on the stovetop over medium heat. Add the salmon fillet pieces and sear, skin side up, for about 2 minutes or until light golden in colour. Remove the salmon and set aside.

Add the extra virgin olive oil to the casserole dish. Add the onion and sauté for about 5 minutes or until softened. Return the salmon, skin side down, to the casserole dish and add the cider, chilli, clams, mussels and half the parsley. Season with

salt and pepper. Cover and place in the oven for 10 minutes. Remove the salmon and shellfish. Set aside and cover to keep warm. (Leave in any shellfish that have not opened.)

Place the casserole dish back on the stovetop over high heat. Bring to the boil, then reduce the heat to a simmer and cook for 5 minutes, or until the liquid is reduced by half. Discard any shellfish that haven't opened by this stage. Serve the salmon pieces with the sauce and shellfish. Sprinkle with the remaining parsley.

SERVES 4

Coca

Catalan Pizza

Coca, a Catalan pizza, is different from Italian pizza as it is rarely served with the Italian staple cheese and tomato sauce. Traditional fare on the Balearic Islands, its toppings range from fresh summer produce to sugar, anís and dried fig.

DOUGH
435 g (16 oz/3½ cups) plain (all-purpose) flour
1 teaspoon dried yeast
½ teaspoon caster (superfine) sugar
2 tablespoons extra virgin olive oil
2 tablespoons white wine

TOPPING
40 g (1½ oz) butter
2 tablespoons caster (superfine) sugar
1 large red onion, thinly sliced
1 teaspoon sherry vinegar
125 g (5 oz/½ cup) tomato paste (concentrated purée)
6 anchovies, finely chopped

Sift the flour into a stainless steel bowl. Add the yeast to 185 ml (6 fl oz/¾ cup) warm water. Add 1 teaspoon salt, the sugar, oil and wine. Make a well in the flour and add the liquid. Combine until a firm ball is formed. Remove to a lightly floured work surface and knead for 5 minutes, or until the dough becomes smooth. Place back in the bowl, cover with plastic wrap and set aside in a warm place for 1 hour, or until doubled in size.

To make the topping, heat the butter and sugar in a small heavy-based saucepan over low heat. Stir until dissolved. Increase the heat to medium and cook without stirring for about 3 minutes, or until the mixture starts to caramelize. Add the onion and cook over medium heat, stirring regularly, for about 8 minutes or until the onion is lightly golden. Add the sherry vinegar and a large pinch of salt and cook for a further 2 minutes, or until the mixture darkens. Remove from the heat and allow to cool to room temperature.

Preheat the oven to 250°C (500°F/Gas 9). Line a baking tray with baking paper. Roll the dough out into four individual oblongs about 5 mm (¼ in) thick and about 25 cm (10 in) diameter. Top with the tomato paste and the cooled onion topping. Sprinkle with the anchovy. Bake on the prepared tray for 7 minutes, or until the base and topping are golden.

VARIATION: You can substitute the anchovy topping with a tuna version. Drain 185 g (6½ oz) tinned tuna in oil and mix with 2 tablespoons chopped capers, 1 tablespoon each of chopped green and black olives and a squeeze of lemon juice. Season to taste.

SERVES 4

CALAMARES RELLENOS CON ARROZ

Stuffed Squid with Rice

This is another example of the glorious rice dishes to be found in Spain. Here, short-grained rice is teamed with sweet, plump little squid stuffed with currants and pine nuts, providing not only a great taste, but a pleasing combinaton of textures.

8 small squid, cleaned, tentacles reserved
  (see page 117)
1 small red onion
2 tablespoons olive oil
2 tablespoons currants
2 tablespoons pine nuts
25 g (1 oz/⅓ cup) fresh breadcrumbs
1 tablespoon chopped mint
1 tablespoon chopped flat-leaf (Italian) parsley
1 egg, lightly beaten
2 teaspoons plain (all-purpose) flour

SAUCE
1 tablespoon olive oil
1 small onion, finely chopped
1 garlic clove, crushed
60 ml (2 fl oz/¼ cup) dry white wine

400 g (14 oz) tinned chopped tomatoes
1 bay leaf
½ teaspoon caster (superfine) sugar

RICE
1.25 litres (44 fl oz/5 cups) fish stock
60 ml (2 fl oz/¼ cup) olive oil
1 brown onion, finely chopped
3 garlic cloves, crushed
275 g (10 oz/1¼ cups) short-grain rice
¼ teaspoon cayenne pepper
3 teaspoons squid ink, optional
60 ml (2 fl oz/¼ cup) dry white wine
60 ml (2 fl oz/¼ cup) tomato paste (concentrated purée)
2 tablespoons chopped flat-leaf (Italian) parsley

Finely chop the squid tentacles and the onion in a food processor. Heat the oil in a saucepan and cook the currants and pine nuts over low heat for 5 minutes, or until the nuts are browned. Transfer to a bowl. Add the onion mixture to the pan and cook gently for 5 minutes, then stir into the pine nut mixture with the breadcrumbs, herbs and egg. Season with salt and pepper. Stuff into the squid bodies, close the openings and secure with toothpicks. Dust with flour.

To make the sauce, heat the olive oil in a frying pan over low heat. Cook the onion for 8 minutes, or until soft. Stir in the garlic, wine and 125 ml (4 fl oz/½ cup) water. Cook over high heat for 1 minute, then add the tomato, bay leaf and sugar. Season, reduce the heat and simmer for 5 minutes.

Add the squid to the pan in a single layer. Simmer, covered, for 20 minutes, or until tender.

Meanwhile, to make the rice, bring the stock to a simmer in a saucepan. Heat the oil in a large saucepan and cook the onion over low heat until soft. Add the garlic, rice and cayenne. Mix the ink, if using, with 80 ml (3 fl oz/⅓ cup) of the stock, add to the rice with the wine and tomato paste and stir until the liquid has almost evaporated. Add 250 ml (9 fl oz/1 cup) of stock and simmer until this evaporates. Add the remaining stock, a cup at a time, until the rice is tender and creamy. Cover and leave off the heat for 5 minutes. Season. Stir in the parsley. Put the rice on a serving plate, arrange the squid on top and spoon on the sauce.

SERVES 4

ATÚN CON TOMATE
Tuna with Tomato

A traditional Andalucían specialty, taking advantage of the fresh seafood available in the region, this is a simple summer dish, as delicious warm as it is the next day cold with a fresh green salad. Try it with the cheaper and more sustainable albacore tuna.

4 x 200 g (7 oz) tuna steaks
80 ml (3 fl oz/⅓ cup) lemon juice
2 tablespoons chopped flat-leaf (Italian) parsley
170 ml (6 fl oz/⅔ cup) olive oil
1 brown onion, finely chopped
2 garlic cloves, chopped

400 g (14 oz) tinned chopped tomatoes
1 bay leaf
1 teaspoon caster (superfine) sugar
1 teaspoon chopped thyme
plain (all-purpose) flour, for dusting

Combine the tuna steaks with the lemon juice, half the parsley and a large pinch of salt, and leave to marinate for 15 minutes. Preheat the oven to 180°C (350°F/Gas 4).

Heat 80 ml (3 fl oz/⅓ cup) of the olive oil in a saucepan over medium heat and cook the onion and garlic for 5 minutes, or until softened. Add the tomato, bay leaf, sugar, thyme and remaining parsley, and season to taste. Increase the heat to high and cook for 3 minutes, or until some of the liquid has reduced.

Heat the remaining oil in a large frying pan over medium–high heat. Drain the tuna steaks and coat in the flour. Cook for about 3 minutes each side, or until golden, then transfer to a casserole dish. Cover with the tomato sauce and bake for about 15 minutes, or until the tuna flakes easily.

SERVES 4

A short marinating time is all that is needed. Any longer and the fish may toughen.

ESCABECHE

Pickled Fish

An ancient method of preparing and preserving fish by first frying, then dressing with an acidic mixture usually containing vinegar. You can also use citrus instead, such as in this version, which uses orange juice and zest, popular in Spanish cookery.

500 g (1 lb 2 oz) skinless firm white fish fillets
  (such as red mullet, whiting, redfish, garfish)
seasoned plain (all-purpose) flour, for dusting
100 ml (4 fl oz) extra virgin olive oil
1 red onion, thinly sliced
2 garlic cloves, thinly sliced
2 thyme sprigs
1 teaspoon ground cumin

2 spring onions (scallions), finely chopped
1/2 teaspoon finely grated orange zest
60 ml (2 fl oz/1/4 cup) fresh orange juice
185 ml (6 fl oz/3/4 cup) white wine
185 ml (6 fl oz/3/4 cup) white wine vinegar
60 g (2 oz/1/2 cup) pitted green olives, roughly chopped
1/2 teaspoon caster (superfine) sugar

Dust the fish lightly with the seasoned flour, shaking off any excess.

Heat 2 tablespoons of the oil in a frying pan over medium heat and add the fish in batches. Cook the fish for 2–3 minutes on each side until lightly browned and just cooked through (the fish should flake easily when tested with a fork). Remove from the pan and put in a single layer in a large, shallow non-metallic dish.

Heat the remaining oil in the same pan, add the onion and garlic and cook, stirring, over medium heat for 5 minutes, or until soft.

Add the thyme sprigs, cumin and spring onion and stir until fragrant. Add the orange zest, orange juice, wine, vinegar, olives and sugar, and season with pepper, to taste. Bring the mixture to the boil, then pour over the fish. Allow the fish to cool in the liquid, then refrigerate overnight. Serve the pickled fish at room temperature.

SERVES 4

PESCADO A LA SAL
Fish Baked in Salt

This dish, typical to Murcia in southern Spain, is most often seen in Spanish restaurants using gilt head bream (dorada) or sea bass (lubina). A restaurant with a particularly theatrical bent will open the whole fish in its jacket of salt at your table.

1.8 kg (4 lb) whole fish (such as gilt head bream, Blue Eye, jewfish, sea bass, groper), scaled and cleaned
2 lemons, sliced
4 thyme sprigs

1 fennel bulb, thinly sliced
3 kg (6 lb 12 oz) rock salt
allioli (see page 249), to serve (optional)

Preheat the oven to 200°C (400°F/Gas 6). Rinse the fish and pat dry inside and out with paper towel. Put the lemon, thyme sprigs and fennel inside the cavity.

Pack half the salt into a large baking dish and put the fish on top. Cover with the remaining salt, pressing down until the salt is packed firmly around the fish.

Bake the fish for 30–40 minutes, or until a metal skewer inserted into the centre of the fish comes out hot. Sharply tap the salt crust with the end of a wooden spoon to crack it, then carefully remove the salt from the top of the fish. Peel the skin away, ensuring that no salt remains on the flesh. Serve the fish hot or cold with allioli or your choice of accompaniment.

SERVES 4–6

The aromatic ingredients that fill the fish cavity will delicately perfume and flavour the flesh from the inside out.

BACALAO

○○○○○○○○○○○○○○○○○○○○○○○○○○○○○○○○

The story of the dried, salted flesh of the Atlantic cod, Gadus morhua, the traditional and now hard to find form of bacalao (salt cod), is a remarkable tale of seamanship, enterprise and ultimately, environmental disaster. It is a lesson in fishery management we would do well to heed today.

A thousand years ago, Basque fishermen regularly set off in tiny sailing boats from the coast of northern Spain to Newfoundland, off the eastern coast of Canada. It was a distance of some 4,500 kilometres (2,800 miles) through the perilous waters of the north Atlantic. Their original quarry was whales, whale meat considered a delicacy in medieval times. The fishermen soon became aware of another fishery so vast that, as legend had it, you could step off a boat and walk across the water on the back of these fish that were swarming in the icy waters: the Atlantic cod.

These intrepid and enterprising fishermen now had to come up with a way of transporting the fish back to the markets of Europe to capitalize on this potentially very lucrative market. They settled on the same method that they used to preserve whale meat: salting and drying the cod where it was caught. This process requires that the fish be beheaded, split, stacked between layers of salt and then dried. When the fish is reconstituted, it must be soaked so that the salt is expelled.

Sadly, in 1992, after a millennium of exploitation, the vast fisheries off Newfoundland collapsed, and have yet to recover. Bacalao now comes mainly from Norway and, no longer a cheap staple, is an expensive ingredient for connoisseurs. The common ling (Molva molva), a fish which has always been sold salted, is now being sold as bacalao.

Cooking with bacalao is not a straightforward process. First you must choose a well-cured piece of cod. It should be white, flexible meat with dark skin, ideally still on, have a unique smell and is best when bought from Spanish or Portuguese sources. The best cuts are the thick steaks from under the belly.

Preparing bacalao for cooking is a good indication of the quality of the salted fish. If, after submerging it in water for 20 hours, and then poaching it for 45 minutes, it collapses, it is of poor quality. Good-quality bacalao, on the other hand, will emerge smooth, white and flexible, without an overly salty flavour. It is served fried, simmered in a sauce, or used as a filling for empanadas or croquettes.

TXANGURRO

Stuffed Crabs

The Basque word for crab is the name given to this justly celebrated dish of crab stuffed with its own meat, wine and garlic. It is a delicious illustration of the Basque genius for devising dishes that complement the flavour of the central ingredient.

4 live large-bodied crabs (such as centollo or spider), about 750 g (1 lb 10 oz) each
80 ml (3 fl oz/⅓ cup) olive oil
1 white onion, finely chopped
1 garlic clove
125 ml (4 fl oz/½ cup) dry white wine

250 ml (9 fl oz/1 cup) tomato passata (puréed tomato)
¼ teaspoon finely chopped tarragon
2 tablespoons dry breadcrumbs
2 tablespoons chopped flat-leaf (Italian) parsley
40 g (1½ oz) chilled butter, chopped into small pieces

Bring a large saucepan of water to the boil. Stir in 3 tablespoons of salt, then add the crabs. Return to the boil and simmer, uncovered, for 15 minutes. Remove the crabs from the water and cool for 30 minutes. Extract the meat from the legs. Open the body without destroying the upper shell, which is needed for serving, reserving any liquid in a bowl. Take out the meat and chop finely with the leg meat. Scoop out all the brown paste from the shells and mix with the chopped meat.

Heat the oil in a frying pan over medium heat and cook the onion and garlic for 5–6 minutes, or until softened. Stir in the wine and tomato passata.

Simmer for 3–4 minutes, then add any reserved crab liquid. Simmer for a further 3–4 minutes. Add the crabmeat and tarragon, and season with salt and freshly ground black pepper. Simmer for about 5 minutes, or until thick. Discard the garlic.

Preheat the oven to 210°C (415°F/Gas 6–7). Rinse and dry the crab shells. Spoon the crab mixture into the shells, levelling the surface. Combine the breadcrumbs and parsley and sprinkle over the top. Dot with butter and bake for 6–8 minutes, or until the butter melts and the breadcrumbs brown. Serve hot.

SERVES 4

Right: Carefully remove the crabmeat from the shells, reserving the shells for serving.

Far right: The breadcrumb and parsley mixture forms a crunchy crust for the tender crab filling below.

BESUGO AL HORNO

Baked Bream with Capsicum, Chilli and Potatoes

Who said fish can't make a hearty, warming meal? Throughout Spain you will find satisfying dishes like this one that marry fish (usually hake and bacalao) with potatoes, especially in the colder and more arid regions of northern Spain.

1.25 kg (2 lb 12 oz) whole red bream, red snapper
   or porgy, cleaned
1 lemon
60 ml (2 fl oz/¼ cup) olive oil
800 g (1 lb 12 oz) potatoes, thinly sliced
3 garlic cloves, thinly sliced
1 handful finely chopped flat-leaf (Italian) parsley
1 small red onion, thinly sliced

1 small dried red chilli, seeded and finely chopped
1 red capsicum (pepper), cored, seeded and cut into
   thin rings
1 yellow capsicum (pepper), cored, seeded and cut
   into thin rings
2 bay leaves
3–4 thyme sprigs
60 ml (2 fl oz/¼ cup) fino sherry

Cut off and discard the fins from the fish and put the fish in a large non-metallic dish. Cut two thin slices from one end of the lemon and reserve. Squeeze the juice from the rest of the lemon into the cavity of the fish. Add 2 tablespoons of the oil and refrigerate, covered, for 2 hours.

Preheat the oven to 190°C (375°F/Gas 5) and lightly oil a shallow earthenware baking dish large enough to hold the whole fish. Spread half the potatoes on the base and scatter the garlic, parsley, onion, chilli and capsicum on top. Season with salt and pepper. Cover with the rest of the potatoes. Pour in 80 ml (3 fl oz/⅓ cup) water and sprinkle the remaining olive oil over the top. Cover with foil and bake for 1 hour.

Increase the oven temperature to 220°C (425°F/Gas 7). Season the fish inside and out with salt and pepper and put the bay leaves and thyme inside the cavity. Make three or four diagonal slashes on each side of the fish. Nestle the fish into the potatoes. Cut the reserved lemon slices in half and fit these into the slashes on one side of the fish, to resemble fins. Bake, uncovered, for 30 minutes, or until the fish is cooked through and the potatoes are golden and crusty.

Pour the sherry over the fish and return to the oven for 3 minutes. Serve straight from the dish.

SERVES 4–6

Zarzuela

Spicy Seafood Soup

This Catalan fish soup is named after a style of light opera. It incorporates a variety of seafood, and is built around a picada, described as the 'Catalan roux'. A blend of garlic, nuts and bread, a picada is used to give form to, or hold together, dishes.

300 g (11 oz) red mullet fillets
400 g (14 oz) firm white fish fillets
300 g (11 oz) cleaned squid tubes
1.5 litres (52 fl oz/6 cups) fish stock
80 ml (3 fl oz/⅓ cup) olive oil
1 white onion, chopped
6 garlic cloves, chopped
1 small red chilli, chopped
1 teaspoon sweet paprika (pimentón)
pinch of saffron threads
150 ml (5 fl oz) white wine
400 g (14 oz) tinned chopped tomatoes

16 raw prawns (shrimp), peeled and deveined, tails intact
2 tablespoons brandy
24 black mussels, cleaned
1 tablespoon chopped flat-leaf (Italian) parsley, to garnish

PICADA
2 tablespoons olive oil
2 slices day-old bread, cubed
2 garlic cloves
5 whole blanched almonds, toasted
2 tablespoons flat-leaf (Italian) parsley

Cut the fish and squid into 4 cm (1½ in) pieces and refrigerate (until ready to use). Pour the stock into a large saucepan, bring to the boil and boil for 15–20 minutes, or until reduced by half.

To make the picada, heat the olive oil in a frying pan, add the bread and stir for 2–3 minutes, or until golden, adding the garlic for the last minute. Process the bread, garlic, almonds and parsley in a food processor and add enough of the stock to make a smooth paste.

Heat 2 tablespoons of the oil in a large saucepan, add the onion, garlic, chilli and paprika, and cook, stirring, for 1 minute. Add the saffron, white wine, tomato and remaining stock. Bring to the boil, then reduce the heat and leave to simmer.

Heat the remaining olive oil in another frying pan over medium heat and cook the fish and squid for 3–5 minutes or until just opaque. Remove and set aside. Add the prawns and cook for 1 minute, then pour in the brandy. Add the prawn mixture to the fish mixture.

Add the mussels to the hot stock and simmer, covered, for 3–5 minutes, or until opened. Discard any mussels that do not open. Return all of the seafood to the pan, add the picada and stir until the sauce has thickened slightly and the seafood is cooked through. Season to taste. Serve garnished with parsley.

SERVES 6–8

Pulpo Gallego
Galician-style Octopus

Melt-in-the-mouth octopus, red with pimentón and glistening with extra virgin olive oil, makes pulpo gallego a long-standing favourite. It is usually served on a wooden platter. Serve with a Galician ribeiro or similar young wine.

2 medium octopus, approximately 500 g (1 lb 2 oz) each
1 bay leaf
10 black peppercorns

smoked or sweet paprika (pimentón), for sprinkling
2 tablespoons extra virgin olive oil
lemon wedges, to serve

Wash the octopus. Using a small knife, carefully cut between the head and tentacles of the octopus, just below the eyes. Grasp the body of the octopus and push the beak out and up through the centre of the tentacles with your finger. Cut the eyes from the head of the octopus by slicing a small disc off with a sharp knife. Discard the eye section.

To clean the octopus head, carefully slit through one side (taking care not to break the ink sac) and scrape out any guts from inside. Rinse under running water to remove any remaining guts.

Bring a large saucepan of water to the boil. Add the bay leaf, peppercorns, 1 teaspoon salt and the octopus. Reduce the heat and simmer for 1 hour, or until tender. Remove the octopus from the water, drain well and leave for 10 minutes.

Cut the octopus tentacles into 1 cm (½ in) thick slices and cut the head into bite-sized pieces. Arrange on a serving platter and sprinkle with paprika and salt. Drizzle with the olive oil and garnish with lemon wedges.

SERVES 4

Far left: Grasp the octopus body and push the beak through the centre of the tentacles.

Left: Carefully clean the head without piercing the ink sac.

Bacalao al Ajo Arriero

Bacalao with Red Capsicum

Certain combinations of ingredients always work well together. One such combination is that of bacalao (salt cod), red capsicum (pepper) and tomatoes, as this dish happily proves. It's found, in various forms, on tables right throughout Spain.

800 g (1 lb 12 oz) bacalao (salt cod)
2 tablespoons olive oil
1 large white onion, chopped
3 garlic cloves, crushed
½ teaspoon dried chilli flakes
2 teaspoons sweet paprika (pimentón)

125 ml (4 fl oz/½ cup) dry white wine
4 ripe tomatoes, finely chopped
2 tablespoons tomato paste (concentrated purée)
2 red capsicums (peppers), roasted and cut into
  strips (see page 246)
2 tablespoons chopped flat-leaf (Italian) parsley

Soak the bacalao in plenty of cold water for about 20 hours in the fridge, changing the water four or five times to remove excess saltiness.

Add the cod to a saucepan of simmering water and poach it gently for 35 minutes. Drain and leave for 10 minutes, or until cool enough to handle. Remove the skin and flake the fish into large pieces, removing any bones. Transfer the fish pieces to a bowl.

Heat the olive oil in a saucepan over medium heat, add the onion and cook, stirring occasionally, for 5 minutes, or until softened. Add the garlic, chilli

flakes and paprika and cook for 1 minute. Increase the heat to high, add the white wine and simmer for 30 seconds. Reduce the heat, add the tomato and tomato paste and cook, stirring occasionally, for 5 minutes, or until thick.

Add the bacalao, cover and simmer for 5 minutes to heat through. Gently stir in the sliced capsicum and parsley and taste before seasoning with salt. Serve hot.

SERVES 6

ENSALADA DE BACALAO, ATÚN Y ANCHOAS

Salad of Salt Cod, Tuna and Anchovy

A simple, modern dish utilizing three traditional Mediterranean ingredients tossed with tomatoes and olives, creating a substantial salad of various textures and flavours. Try it also with endive replacing the cos or with a vinaigrette.

250 g (9 oz) bacalao (salt cod)
1 bay leaf
20 hazelnuts
20 almonds
125 ml (4 fl oz/½ cup) extra virgin olive oil
2 slices bread, crusts removed and cut into quarters
2 red capsicums (pepper), roasted (see page 246)
4 garlic cloves

2 tablespoons sherry vinegar
2 tablespoons flat-leaf (Italian) parsley, chopped roughly
1 small head cos lettuce
185 g (7 oz) tinned Spanish tuna in oil, drained
6 anchovies, roughly chopped
1 red onion, very finely sliced
16 black olives
2 roma (plum) tomatoes, cut into thin wedges

Desalinate the bacalao by putting it in a large bowl and covering well with cold water. Soak for 20 hours, in the refrigerator, changing the water regularly. Rinse and place in a small saucepan. Cover with water and add the bay leaf. Bring to the boil, then reduce the heat to a simmer and cook for 10 minutes, or until the flesh starts to come away from the bone. Drain and set aside until cool enough to handle, then remove the skin and bones and break the flesh into small flakes. Set aside until ready to use.

Preheat the oven to 180°C (350°F/Gas 4). Spread the nuts out on a baking tray and roast for about 5 minutes, or until light golden. Cool, then remove the skins from the hazelnuts by rubbing together in a clean tea towel (dish towel).

Heat 2 tablespoons of the olive oil in a frying pan over medium heat. Fry the bread pieces until light golden, about 1 minute, on each side. Drain on paper towel and allow to cool. Place the roasted capsicum, nuts, remaining oil, fried bread, garlic, sherry vinegar and parsley into a food processor and process until smooth. Season the dressing with at least 1 teaspoon of salt.

Wash and dry the lettuce. Tear and arrange on plates. Arrange the bacalao, tuna, anchovies, onion, olives and tomato decoratively over the lettuce. Serve with the dressing.

SERVES 4

PAELLA MARINERA
Seafood Rice

Paella is the dish by which Spanish food is defined internationally. It originated in the rice-growing Ebro River delta area, inland from the city of Valencia in the east of Spain, but now firmly belongs, with delicious seafood added, to the whole country.

12 black mussels
125 ml (4 fl oz/½ cup) white wine
1 red onion, chopped
125 ml (4 fl oz/½ cup) olive oil
½ red onion, extra, finely chopped
1 thick slice of jamón, finely chopped
4 garlic cloves, crushed
1 red capsicum (pepper), finely chopped
1 ripe tomato, peeled, seeded and chopped
  (see page 246)

90 g (3 oz) chorizo, thinly sliced
pinch of cayenne pepper
220 g (8 oz/1 cup) paella or medium-grain rice
¼ teaspoon saffron threads
500 ml (17 fl oz/2 cups) chicken stock, heated
85 g (3 oz/½ cup) fresh or frozen peas
12 raw prawns (shrimp), peeled and deveined
2 squid tubes, cleaned and cut into rings
115 g (4 oz) skinless firm white fish fillets, cut into pieces
2 tablespoons finely chopped flat-leaf (Italian) parsley

Scrub the mussels and remove the hairy beards. Discard any open mussels or those that don't close when tapped on the bench.

Heat the wine and red onion in a saucepan over high heat. Add the mussels, cover and gently shake the pan for 5–8 minutes. Remove from the heat and discard any closed mussels. Drain, reserving the liquid.

Heat the oil in a large heavy-based frying pan, add the extra onion, jamón, garlic and capsicum, and cook for 5 minutes. Add the chopped tomato, chorizo and cayenne pepper. Season. Stir in the reserved liquid, then add the rice and stir again.

Blend the saffron with the hot stock, then stir into the rice mixture. Bring to the boil, then reduce the heat to low and simmer, uncovered, for 15 minutes without stirring.

Put the peas, prawns, squid and fish pieces on top of the rice. Push them in, cover and cook over low heat for 10 minutes, turning over halfway through, until the rice is tender and the seafood is cooked through. Add the mussels for the last 5 minutes to heat through. If the rice is not quite cooked, add a little extra stock and cook for a few more minutes. Leave to rest for 5 minutes, then add the parsley and serve.

SERVES 4

SARDINAS MURCIANAS
Sardines Murcia Style

All along the Murcian coast, in Spain's south-east, sardines are landed and transported, still flapping, to kitchens along the seafront. With seafood, freshness is paramount, but this is especially so for Spain's much-loved sardina.

24 fresh large sardines, cleaned, with backbones,
    heads and tails removed
1 kg (2 lb 4 oz) ripe tomatoes, peeled and seeded
    (see page 246)
2 green capsicums (peppers), cored, seeded and cut
    into thin rings
1 white onion, sliced into thin rings

2 all-purpose potatoes, cut into 5 mm (¼ in) slices
2 tablespoons chopped flat-leaf (Italian) parsley
3 garlic cloves, crushed
¼ teaspoon saffron threads, lightly toasted
2 tablespoons olive oil
chopped flat-leaf (Italian) parsley, extra, to garnish

Preheat the oven to 180°C (350°F/Gas 4). Lightly oil a large, shallow earthenware or ceramic baking dish that is wide enough to hold the length of the sardines. Open out the sardines and then lightly sprinkle the insides with salt. Fold them back into their original shape.

Cut each prepared tomato into thin slices. Cover the base of the baking dish with a third of the tomato slices. Layer half the salted sardines on top. Follow this with a layer of half the capsicum, then half the onion, then half the potato slices. Sprinkle with half the parsley and garlic, and season with freshly ground black pepper. Crumble half the saffron over the top.

Layer the remaining sardines, half the remaining tomatoes and then the other ingredients as before. Finish with the last of the tomatoes. Season well with salt and freshly ground black pepper. Drizzle the oil over the surface and cover with foil. Bake for 1 hour, or until the potatoes are cooked. Spoon off any excess liquid, sprinkle with parsley and serve straight from the dish.

SERVES 6

Far left: Sprinkle the salt over the cleaned sardines before folding them back into their original shape.

Left: The sardines are cooked to perfection amongst the layers of vegetables.

TRUCHA CON JAMÓN
Trout with Jamón

The cold mountain rivers of Navarra teem with trout, which are caught for sport and eating. This recipe, often called Trucha a la Navarra, uses bacon fat as the cooking medium, olive oil being formerly an expensive luxury for the cooks of Navarra.

4 x 200 g (7 oz) river trout, cleaned and deboned
80 g (3 oz/1 bunch) mint, broken into sprigs
185 ml (6 fl oz/¾ cup) white wine
8 slices jamón or prosciutto

2 tablespoons bacon fat
2 tablespoons lemon juice
40 g (1½ oz) chilled butter, chopped

Stuff each trout cavity with several sprigs of mint. Arrange in a dish in which they fit together snugly and drizzle with the wine. Cover and marinate in the refrigerator for at least 6 hours.

Preheat the oven to 180°C (350°F/Gas 4). Remove the fish from the marinade and pat dry, reserving the marinade. Remove the mint from each trout cavity and discard. Season the cavity. Roll up two pieces of jamón per fish and put in the cavity with some more mint sprigs.

Heat the bacon fat in a frying pan over medium heat for 4 minutes, or until melted. Add the fish and fry for 3 minutes each side, or until crisp.

Transfer the fish to an ovenproof dish and bake for about 10 minutes, or until the fish is no longer translucent and can be flaked easily with a fork.

Meanwhile, combine the reserved marinade and lemon juice in the frying pan and boil over high heat for about 5 minutes, or until the sauce reduces to a syrupy consistency. Gradually whisk in the butter until the sauce is glossy. Serve the fish with the jamón and mint inside, drizzled with the sauce.

SERVES 4

Far left: The marinated fish is stuffed with the jamón and mint sprigs before cooking.

Left: Ensure that you gradually whisk in the butter so the sauce doesn't separate, becoming oily.

CALAMARES A LA PLANCHA
Pan-fried Calamari

'A la plancha' means 'cooking on a hot flat plate', as opposed to 'a la parilla', which means 'on the grill'. A la plancha is a favourite method in many tapas bars, and calamari prepared this way – sweet, tender and lightly charred – are especially good.

500 g (1 lb 2 oz) small squid
2 tablespoons olive oil

PICADA
2 tablespoons extra virgin olive oil
2 tablespoons finely chopped flat-leaf (Italian) parsley
1 garlic clove, crushed

To clean the squid, gently pull the tentacles away from the tube (the intestines should come away at the same time). Remove the intestines from the tentacles by cutting under the eyes, then remove the beak if it remains in the centre of the tentacles by using your fingers to push up the centre. Pull away the soft bone from the hood.

Rub the tubes under cold running water. The skin should come away easily. Wash the hoods and tentacles and drain well. Transfer to a bowl, add ¼ teaspoon salt and mix well. Cover and refrigerate for 30 minutes.

Close to serving time, whisk the picada ingredients with ¼ teaspoon ground black pepper and some salt in a bowl.

Heat the olive oil in a frying pan over high heat and cook the squid hoods in small batches for 2–3 minutes, or until the hoods turn white and are tender. Cook the squid tentacles, turning to brown them all over, for 1 minute, or until they curl up. Serve hot, drizzled with the picada.

PICTURE ON PAGE 118

SERVES 4

Right: Gently pull out the tentacles and intestines, then the quill or soft bone.

Far right: The skin should come away easily when the squid tubes are run under cold water.

Pan-fried Calamari (recipe on page 117)

DEL 13 AL 17 DE JUNIO 2007

Plaza Toros de COLLADO VILLALBA

Empresa: EXCMO. AYUNTAMIENTO - Organiza: COMISION DE MAYORDOMOS Y TOMAS ENTERO, S.L. - Colabora: PEDRO SANTAM

FERIA TAURINA DE SAN ANTONIO

se celebrarán, si el tiempo no lo impide, con permiso de la Autoridad y bajo su presidencia.

5 SENSACIONALES ACONTECIMIENTOS TAURINOS, 5

MIERCOLES 13 7 TARDE — NOVILLADA SIN PICADORES

6 HERMOSOS NOVILLOS **Toros de Triana**
señal, hoja de higuera en la dcha, orejana una divisa, azul cielo y blanca, de la ganadería de de CASTILLO DE LAS GUARDAS (Sevilla), para los valientes novilleros **ESPADAS**

JERONIMO DELGADO - MIGUEL NAVARRO - PABLO LECHUGA
acompañados de sus correspondientes cuadrillas

VIERNES 15 7 TARDE — NOVILLADA SIN PICADORE

6 HERMOSOS NOVILLOS Dª Pilar y D. Tomás Entero Granero
sello descuartado la dcha. y mosca en la uñi divisa, roja y blanca, de la ganadería de de COLMENAREJO (Madrid), para los valientes novilleros **ESPADAS**

JUAN CARLOS REY - TOMAS CERQUEIRA - JUAN CARLOS CABELLO
acompañados de sus correspondientes cuadrillas

SABADO 16 7 TARDE — NOVILLADA CON PICADORES
6 BRAVOS NOVILLOS-TOROS **Hnos. González**
de COLLADO VILLALBA (Madrid), para los valientes novilleros **ESPADAS**

CARLOS GUZMAN

DOMINGO 17 7 TARDE — GRAN CORRIDA DE TOROS

6 SOBERBIOS TOROS **Hnos. Garzón Mergelina**
serial, hoja de higuera en la dcha. divisa: roja y amarilla de la ganadería de de SANTA OLALLA DE CALA (Huelva), para los sensacionales matadores de toros **ESPADAS**

VICTOR JANEIRO

Chapter 3

HOME COOKING

Spain's rich history is no more apparent than in *comida casera*, the food the Spanish enjoy at home. This food is imprinted with the passionate spirit of the peoples who have invaded Spain over many centuries.

DULCE DE MEMBRILLO

Quince Paste

A Spanish standby. Not only sweet, this fruit paste is wonderful served with a good Manchego, Roncal or Idiazábal cheese – even a strong blue – at breakfast on toast, in salads, or for the merienda (afternoon snack).

3 large quinces
caster (superfine) sugar

Wash the quinces, place in a saucepan, cover with water and simmer for 30 minutes, or until tender. Drain. Peel and core the quinces then push them through a sieve or potato ricer. Weigh the quince pulp, place in a heavy-based saucepan and add the same weight of sugar.

Cook over low heat, stirring occasionally with a wooden spoon, for 3½–4½ hours, or until thick.

Pour into a shallow 28 x 18 cm (11 x 7 inch) rectangular tin, or several smaller moulds, lined with plastic wrap. Allow to cool.

Quince paste can be kept for several months in a tightly sealed container. Serve with cheese, or with game such as pheasant.

MAKES 1 BLOCK 28 CM X 18 CM

Ajo Blanco
Chilled Almond Soup

Your first encounter with this cool, silky-smooth soup with pale-green grapes and croutons floating on top will astonish and delight you. Another version of gazpacho, ajo blanco is a survivor of the medieval Moorish cuisine of the Mediterranean.

200 g (7 oz) day-old white crusty bread, crusts removed
155 g (6 oz/1 cup) whole blanched almonds
3–4 garlic cloves, chopped
125 ml (4 fl oz/½ cup) extra virgin olive oil
80 ml (3 fl oz/⅓ cup) sherry vinegar
310–375 ml (11–13 fl oz/1¼–1½ cups) vegetable or chicken stock

2 tablespoons olive oil
75 g (3 oz) day-old white crusty bread, extra, crusts removed, cut into 1 cm (½ in) cubes
200 g (7 oz) small seedless green grapes
aged sherry vinegar, for serving

Soak the bread in cold water for 5 minutes, then squeeze out any excess liquid. Process the almonds and garlic in a food processor until well ground. Add the bread and process until smooth.

With the motor running, add the extra virgin olive oil in a steady slow stream until the mixture is the consistency of thick mayonnaise (add a little water if the mixture is too thick). Slowly add the sherry vinegar and 310 ml (11 fl oz/1¼ cups) of the stock. Blend for 1 minute. Season with salt. Refrigerate for at least 2 hours. The soup will thicken on refrigeration so you may need to add stock or water to thin it.

When ready to serve, heat the olive oil in a frying pan, add the bread cubes and toss over medium heat for 2–3 minutes, or until golden. Drain on paper towel. Serve the soup very cold. Garnish with the grapes and bread cubes and sprinkle with aged sherry vinegar if desired.

SERVES 4–6

GAZPACHO

Chilled Tomato Soup

The Andalucíans have devised many ways to deal with the searing heat of their summers, not the least of them, the cold soup. Gazpacho, the most famous of these wonderfully refreshing soups, is simplicity itself to make – and even easier to eat.

2 slices day-old white crusty bread, crusts removed, broken into pieces
1 kg (2 lb 4 oz) vine-ripened tomatoes, peeled, seeded and chopped (see page 246)
1 red capsicum (pepper), seeded, roughly chopped
2 garlic cloves, chopped
1 small green chilli, chopped (optional)
1 teaspoon caster (superfine) sugar
2 tablespoons red wine vinegar
2 tablespoons extra virgin olive oil

GARNISH
½ Lebanese (short) cucumber, seeded, finely diced
½ red capsicum (pepper), seeded, finely diced
½ green capsicum (pepper), seeded, finely diced
½ red onion, finely diced
½ ripe tomato, diced

Soak the bread in cold water for 5 minutes, then squeeze out any excess liquid. Put the bread in a food processor with the tomato, capsicum, garlic, chilli, sugar and vinegar, and process until well combined and smooth.

With the motor running, gradually add the oil to make a smooth creamy mixture. Season to taste. Refrigerate for at least 2 hours. Add a little extra red wine vinegar, if desired.

To make the garnish, mix together the ingredients. Spoon the chilled gazpacho into soup bowls, top with a little of the garnish and serve the remaining garnish in separate bowls on the side.

SERVES 4

Far left: Use a teaspoon to scoop out the cucumber seeds before dicing the flesh.

Left: Squeeze the excess water from the soaked bread.

Pure de Vigilia

Lenten Soup

Semana Santa (Easter) is an important festival in Spain, and for the many Catholic Spaniards who do not consume meat during Lent, this is a good alternative. It certainly doesn't have to be a hardship with this rich purée of chickpeas and potatoes.

250 g (9 oz) bacalao (salt cod)
250 g (9 oz) chickpeas
1 leek, white part only
1 red onion
2 carrots

1 green capsicum (pepper)
2 floury potatoes
80 ml (3 fl oz/ 1/3 cup) olive oil
2 garlic cloves, chopped
1/2 teaspoon sweet paprika (pimentón)

Put the bacalao in a large bowl and cover with cold water. Refrigerate for 20 hours, changing the water several times during the soaking process. Put the chickpeas in a separate bowl, cover with cold water and soak overnight.

Roughly chop the leek, onion, carrots, capsicum and potatoes.

Heat the olive oil in a large, heavy-based saucepan over medium heat. Sauté the onion, garlic, leek and carrot until softened, about 5 minutes. Add the drained chickpeas and bacalao and 1.5 litres (52 fl oz/6 cups) of water. Bring to the boil, then cover, reduce the heat and simmer for 30 minutes.

After 30 minutes, carefully remove the bacalao. When cool enough to handle, remove the skin and bones and return the flesh in large pieces back to the pan and continue simmering for a further 30 minutes. Add the potato, capsicum and paprika. Continue to cook for another 30 minutes or until the potato is soft.

Cool slightly, then blend in a food processor, in batches, until smooth. Season to taste, then gently reheat if necessary. Add more water if you prefer a thinner soup.

PICTURE ON PAGE 130

SERVES 4–6

When the bacalao is cooked and cooled, separate the flesh from the skin and bones before returning the flesh to the pan.

Lenten Soup (recipe on page 129)

CALDO GALLEGO
Galician-style Soup

This dish is served and cooked in all Galician restaurants, and in most Galician homes during the winter months. It can accommodate as many different ingredients as there are cooks making it.

250 g (9 oz/1¼ cups) dried white haricot beans
  (such as navy beans)
500 g (1 lb 2 oz) smoked ham hock
2 tablespoons olive oil
1 leek, chopped
1 garlic clove, chopped

500 g (1 lb 2 oz) pork baby back or American-style ribs,
  separated into 5 cm (2 in) widths
2 all-purpose potatoes, peeled and cubed
1 bay leaf
1 kg (2 lb 4 oz/1 bunch) silverbeet (Swiss chard),
  washed well and chopped

Rinse the beans, then soak them in cold water for at least 5 hours.

Put the ham hock in a large heavy-based saucepan and cover with cold water. Bring to the boil, then reduce the heat and simmer for about 1 hour, or until the meat is tender and starts to come away from the bone. Remove from the heat. When the hock is cool enough to handle, remove the meat from the bone and cut into 2 cm (³/4 in) cubes. Reserve 625 ml (22 fl oz/2½ cups) of the liquid.

Put the beans in a large saucepan and cover with cold water. Bring to the boil, then reduce the heat and simmer for 30 minutes, or until tender. Drain, reserving 250 ml (9 fl oz/1 cup) of the liquid.

Heat the olive oil in a large heavy-based saucepan over medium heat and cook the leek and garlic for about 5 minutes, or until translucent. Add the chopped ham, beans, pork or ribs, potato, bay leaf and reserved cooking liquid (make sure the food is covered with liquid). Bring to the boil, then reduce the heat, cover and simmer for 45 minutes. Stir in the silverbeet and cook for 5 minutes. Season before serving.

SERVES 4

The dried beans need to be soaked before use, but you can use pre-cooked white beans if you are short on time. Simply skip the first step in the method.

GARBANZOS Y ACELGAS

Chickpeas and Silverbeet

This quick and easy recipe is great as an accompaniment to a heavier main dish, or as a tasty, nutritious vegetarian alternative, with silverbeet adding a distinctive flavour. Popular in Cádiz, on the Andalucían Atlantic coast, during Semana Santa, Easter.

250 g (9 oz) dried chickpeas
1 carrot, diced
1 sprig flat-leaf (Italian) parsley
1 bay leaf
2 brown onions, chopped
80 ml (3 fl oz/⅓ cup) extra virgin olive oil

1 garlic clove, chopped
2 tomatoes, chopped
250 g (9 oz) silverbeet (Swiss chard), washed well
   and chopped
2 hard-boiled eggs, peeled and chopped

Put the chickpeas in a bowl, cover with cold water and soak overnight.

Drain and rinse the chickpeas and put in a large saucepan with the carrot, parsley, bay leaf and half the chopped onion. Cover with 750 ml (26 fl oz/ 3 cups) of water, then bring to the boil and cook for about 20 minutes, or until almost tender. Add 2 teaspoons salt and half the oil and cook for a further 10 minutes.

Heat the remaining olive oil in a frying pan over medium heat and cook the garlic and remaining onion for 5 minutes, or until softened. Add the tomato and cook for 5 minutes.

Stir the tomato mixture into the chickpea mixture (it should be wet enough to be saucy but not too soupy). Stir in the silverbeet. Cook for 5 minutes, or until the silverbeet is tender. Season well and serve topped with the boiled egg.

SERVES 4

Right: When the tomato and chickpea mixtures are combined, they should be thick and saucy.

Far right: The silverbeet needs to cook until it is just wilted and tender.

PATATAS A LA IMPORTANCIA
Widowed Potatoes

This an old dish, whose name translates directly to 'important potatoes' because it uses a humble ingredient as a centrepiece. It is more often called 'widowed potatoes' in modern-day Spain because it contains no meat or fish.

500 ml (17 fl oz/2 cups) extra virgin olive oil,
   for shallow frying
3 large all-purpose potatoes (such as desiree),
   cut into 1cm (½ in) slices
3 eggs, beaten
plain (all-purpose) flour for coating and thickening

4 garlic cloves, finely chopped
2 small brown onions, finely chopped
4 small tomatoes, peeled, seeded and finely chopped
   (see page 246)
1 teaspoon caster (superfine) sugar
400 ml (14 fl oz) beef stock

Preheat the oven to 160°C (315°F/Gas 2–3). Heat the oil in a frying pan over medium–high heat.

Dip the potato slices in the beaten egg, then the flour. Fry until golden on both sides, 2 minutes per side. Transfer to a heatproof casserole or baking dish.

Add the garlic and onion to the frying pan and cook for 5 minutes over medium heat, or until softened, then add the chopped tomato and cook over low heat until it reduces slightly. Add the sugar and stir to combine.

Sprinkle ½ teaspoon of flour over the mixture, stir through until it is smooth, then pour over the potato. Gently pour over the stock and season with a little salt. Cover and bake for 45 minutes, then uncover and cook for a further 15 minutes, or until the potato is tender.

SERVES 4

Dip the potato slices in the beaten egg and flour before frying until golden.

GUISANTES A LA VALENCIANA

Valencian Peas

The river delta regions around Valencia are famed for rice and the huertas (market gardens). This simple but tasty dish is best made with the freshest baby peas in season. Particularly delicious when served with roast lamb or pork.

a pinch of saffron threads
2 tablespoons white wine
2 tablespoons olive oil
1 small onion, finely diced
1 garlic clove, crushed

¼ teaspoon ground cumin
125 ml (4 fl oz/½ cup) chicken stock
1 bay leaf
310 g (11 oz/2 cups) fresh or frozen peas
2 tablespoons chopped flat-leaf (Italian) parsley

Soak the saffron in the wine for 10 minutes to help bring out the colour. Heat the oil in a saucepan over medium heat. Sauté the onion, garlic and cumin for about 2–3 minutes, or until the onion is translucent. Add the saffron wine mixture, stock, bay leaf and peas. Season with salt and pepper.

Bring to the boil, then reduce to a steady simmer. Cook, uncovered, for 5 minutes, or until the peas are cooked and the liquid has evaporated. Sprinkle with the chopped parsley and season to taste.

SERVES 4 AS A SIDE

Soaking the saffron in the wine before you start will help to bring out its colour and flavour.

ESCALIVADA

Barbecued Vegetable Salad

Escalivar is a Catalan verb meaning to cook in hot ashes or embers, which is how escalivada, this flavoursome vegetable salad, is best prepared. Lacking ashes or embers, it works well when cooked on a barbecue and assembled with fried capers.

1 red onion
6 small eggplants (aubergines), about 16 cm
  (6¼ in) long
4 red capsicums (peppers)
4 orange capsicums (peppers)

1 tablespoon baby capers, rinsed and drained
80 ml (3 fl oz/⅓ cup) olive oil
1 tablespoon chopped flat-leaf (Italian) parsley
2 garlic cloves, finely chopped

Without slicing through the base, cut the red onion from top to bottom into six sections. Put on a barbecue, or over an open-flamed grill or gas stovetop with the eggplants and capsicums. Cook the vegetables over medium heat for 10 minutes, turning occasionally, until the eggplant and capsicum skins are blackened and blistered. Put the capsicums in a plastic bag for 10 minutes to cool. Set aside the onion and eggplant.

Dry-fry the capers with a pinch of salt until crisp. Separate the onion into its six sections and discard the charred outer skins. Peel the skins off the eggplants and remove the stalks. Cut the eggplants from top to bottom into slices. Peel the capsicums and remove the seeds. Cut the capsicums into wide slices.

Arrange all the vegetables on a large platter. Drizzle the olive oil over the top and season with salt and pepper. Scatter the parsley, garlic and capers over the top. Serve cold as a salad or warm as an accompaniment to barbecued meats.

SERVES 4

Right: Leave the base of the red onion intact, then cut the onion into six sections.

Far right: Char the onion over an open flame.

Huevos a la Flamenca

Baked Eggs

This dish is originally from Andalucía, but is now found right around the Spanish peninsula. It is full of the colour, gutsy flavours and exuberance of the gypsies who invented flamenco. Serve it with a big glass of grenache from Alicante.

80 ml (3 fl oz/⅓ cup) olive oil
400 g (14 oz) potatoes, cut into 2 cm (¾ in) cubes
1 red capsicum (pepper), cut into thin strips
1 brown onion, chopped
100 g (4 oz) thinly sliced jamón or prosciutto
150 g (6 oz) thin green asparagus spears, trimmed
100 g (4 oz) fresh or frozen green peas

100 g (4 oz) baby green beans, sliced
500 g (1 lb 2 oz) ripe tomatoes, peeled, seeded and chopped (see page 246)
2 tablespoons tomato paste (concentrated purée)
4 eggs
100 g (4 oz) chorizo, thinly sliced
2 tablespoons chopped flat-leaf (Italian) parsley

Heat the oil in a large frying pan and cook the potato over medium heat for 8 minutes, or until golden. Remove with a slotted spoon. Reduce the heat and add the capsicum and onion to the pan. Cut two of the jamón slices into pieces similar in size to the capsicum and add to the pan. Cook for 6 minutes, or until the onion is soft.

Preheat the oven to 180°C (350°F/Gas 4). Reserve four asparagus spears. Add the rest to the pan with the peas, beans, tomato and tomato paste. Stir in 125 ml (4 fl oz/½ cup) water and season well with salt and freshly ground black pepper. Return the potato to the pan. Cover and cook over low heat for 10 minutes, stirring occasionally.

Grease a large oval ovenproof dish. Transfer the vegetables to the dish, discarding any excess liquid. Using the back of a spoon, make four deep, evenly spaced indentations and break an egg into each. Top with the reserved asparagus and the chorizo. Cut the remaining jamón into large pieces and distribute over the top. Sprinkle with parsley. Bake for about 20 minutes, or until the egg whites are just set. Serve warm.

SERVES 4

Right: Return the fried potato to the pan with the other vegetables, cover and cook until tender.

Far right: Carefully break the eggs into the indentations on top of the vegetable mixture.

Patatas a lo Pobre

Poor Man's Potatoes

This is another delicious recipe from la cocina pobre – the cuisine of the poor – that would be at home on even the richest of tables. It is particularly wonderful when served with baked lamb.

4 large all-purpose potatoes, such as desiree,
   approximately 800 g (1 lb 12 oz) in total
250 ml (9 fl oz/1 cup) light olive oil

250 ml (9 fl oz/1 cup) extra virgin olive oil
1 green capsicum (pepper), diced into 2 cm (³/₄ in) cubes
1 red onion, diced into 2 cm (³/₄ in) cubes

Peel and cut the potatoes into 1 cm (¹/₂ in) thick slices and soak in cold water for 20 minutes. Drain well and dry on paper towel.

Heat the oils in a large, deep heavy-based frying pan over medium–high heat. When the oil is hot, add the potatoes and 1 teaspoon salt. Fry on high heat for 10 minutes, rotating and turning potatoes regularly until lightly golden. Reduce the heat to low, cover with a lid and cook for 10 minutes, or until starting to soften.

Add the capsicum and onion cubes, stirring well. Cover and cook for a further 10 minutes, stirring occasionally to prevent the vegetables sticking. Increase the heat to high and cook, uncovered, for another 15 minutes. When cooked the potatoes will be tender and have broken up slightly but will be a little crispy on the edges. Drain well. Season to taste and serve hot.

SERVES 4–6

Add the onion and capsicum when the potatoes are lightly golden.

Food Journey

WINE

oooooooooooooooooooooooooooooooooooooooo

In Spain you find two tendencies side by side: a willingness to experiment and an understanding of the importance of tradition. Combined with a wide range of soils and climatic conditions, they produce an extraordinary range of wine styles.

While racing into the bright future, Spanish winemakers have not jettisoned the fine traditions of the past. Sherry is a prime example. Before the days of tight corks and glass bottles, when air invaded wine, the obvious answer was to develop a taste for oxidized wines: rancio. In Jerez, this technique was refined and improved until it became what it is today, a wine style that is among the most sought after in the world.

In the dry heat of Andalucía, in addition to sherry, you will find the cool-fermented fruity white wines of Condado de Huelva; in the Rías Baixas region of Galicia, the classic white wine of Spain, made using the Albariño grape; and in Málaga, rich sweet wines made using the Pedro Ximénez grape.

The list of quality Spanish wines goes on: the magnificent cavas, the sparkling wines of Catalonia; the famed Vega Sicilia, the standard bearer for the Ribero del Duero region; and the celebrated red wines that are made mainly from the indigenous tempranillo grape in the Rioja.

Today the various Spanish wines are produced in 17 autonomías – autonomous regions – divided into 50 provinces. Every year, a new autonomía will seize the interest of the wine world and an old denomination will learn some new tricks, like Jumilla in Murcia.

With the largest area of land dedicated to viticulture in the world, the Spanish wine industry is of immense importance to Spain's economy. The varied climatic conditions and diverse countryside in the Iberian Peninsula contributes to the strength of the industry as the moderate conditions are perfect for most grapes, and you'll see vineyards dotted across the countryside.

The winemaking industry is another in Spain that has benefited from the Denomiación de Origen initiative (D.O.), ensuring that wine production is regulated and that quality remains high. With the range of quality Spanish wines that have become available, and improved marketing and distribution, they are not only enjoyed in the restaurants and tascas of Spain, but increasingly in overseas markets as well.

TUMBET

Baked Layered Vegetables

The classic vegetable dish of Mallorca, tumbet is eaten as a meal in its own right, either hot or cold, or as an accompaniment to dishes like baked lampuga (in English, mahi mahi or dolphin fish) enjoyed during its short Mediterranean autumn season.

TOMATO SAUCE
2 tablespoons olive oil
3 garlic cloves, crushed
1 red onion, finely chopped
1 kg (2 lb 4 oz) ripe tomatoes, peeled, seeded
   and chopped (see page 246)
2 teaspoons chopped thyme

250 ml (9 fl oz/1 cup) olive oil
500 g (1 lb 2 oz) all-purpose potatoes (such as desiree,
   kipfler or pontiac), cut into 5 mm (¼ in) rounds

500 g (1 lb 2 oz) eggplants (aubergines), cut into
   5 mm (¼ in) rounds
500 g (1 lb 2 oz) green capsicums (peppers), seeded
   and cut into 3 cm (1¼ in) pieces
1 handful flat-leaf (Italian) parsley, roughly chopped
allioli (see page 249), to serve (optional)

To make the tomato sauce, heat the olive oil in a heavy-based frying pan and cook the garlic and onion over low heat for 6–8 minutes, or until softened. Increase the heat to medium, add the tomato and thyme and cook for 20 minutes, or until thickened. Season to taste. Preheat the oven to 180°C (350°F/Gas 4).

While the sauce is cooking, heat half the oil in a heavy-based frying pan over low heat and cook the potato rounds in batches until tender but not brown. Remove with a slotted spoon or tongs and transfer to a casserole dish measuring about 27 x 21 x 5 cm (10¾ x 8¼ x 2 in). Season lightly with salt and freshly ground black pepper.

Increase the heat to high and cook the eggplant for 3 minutes each side, or until golden, adding a little more oil as necessary. Drain the slices on paper towel, then arrange on top of the potatoes. Season lightly.

Cook the capsicum in the same pan until tender but not browned, about 5 minutes, adding a little more olive oil as needed. Remove with a slotted spoon, drain on paper towel and arrange over the eggplant. Season lightly. Pour the sauce over the top and bake for 20 minutes, or until hot and bubbling. Serve warm, sprinkled with parsley, to accompany fish or meat, or at room temperature with allioli.

SERVES 6–8

PIMIENTOS RELLENOS
Stuffed Capsicums

Many vegetable dishes thought of by non-Spaniards as 'sides' will turn up in Spanish homes as dishes in their own right. This is especially true of the vegetables of Navarra, La Rioja, and regions across the country's north, which are famed throughout Spain.

4 red capsicums (peppers)
60 ml (2 fl oz/¼ cup) olive oil
1 brown onion, chopped
2 garlic cloves, chopped
400 g (14 oz) minced (ground) pork or lamb

125 ml (4 fl oz/½ cup) white wine
400 g (14 oz) tinned chopped tomatoes, drained well
100 g (4 oz) rice, cooked
1 egg, lightly beaten
2 tablespoons finely chopped flat-leaf (Italian) parsley

Cut the tops off the capsicums and reserve them to use as lids. Using a small, sharp knife, carefully cut the internal membrane and seeds away from the capsicum and discard. Preheat the oven to 180°C (350°F/Gas 4).

Heat 2 tablespoons of the olive oil in a frying pan over medium–high heat and cook the onion and garlic for 5 minutes, or until lightly golden. Add the pork or lamb and brown well. Stir in the wine, then reduce the heat to low and simmer for about 10 minutes, or until the wine has been absorbed.

Add the drained tomato and simmer for a further 10 minutes, then add the rice. Remove from the heat and stir in the egg and parsley. Season well.

Stuff the capsicums with the meat mixture, put the lids on top and stand upright in an ovenproof dish. Drizzle with the remaining olive oil and bake for 45–50 minutes, or until the capsicums are tender and the stuffing is cooked through. Remove from the oven and leave, covered, for about 5 minutes before serving.

SERVES 4

Right: Prepare the capsicums by removing the tops and the inner membranes and seeds.

Far right: Spoon the filling into the capsicums before replacing the tops and drizzling with olive oil.

Fideos a la Catalana

Catalan Noodles

There are numerous recipes for this noodle dish, a curiosity of Catalan cuisine. Unlike most Italian pastas, fideos are very short – half the length of your little finger – and thin, more noodle than spaghetti. Below is a classic combination of fideos with pork.

80 ml (3 fl oz/⅓ cup) olive oil

250 g (9 oz) pork spare ribs, cut into 1 cm (½ in) thick slices

1 brown onion, chopped

125 ml (4 fl oz/½ cup) tomato passata (puréed tomato)

1 teaspoon sweet paprika (pimentón)

100 g (4 oz) fresh spicy pork sausages, thickly sliced

100 g (4 oz) chorizo, sliced

1.5 litres (52 fl oz/6 cups) beef or chicken stock

500 g (1 lb 2 oz) spaghettini, broken into 2.5 cm (1 in) pieces

PICADA

50 g (2 oz/⅓ cup) nuts (either hazelnuts, pine nuts or almonds)

2 garlic cloves, crushed

2 tablespoons chopped flat-leaf (Italian) parsley

¼ teaspoon ground cinnamon

1 slice bread, toasted and crusts removed

¼ teaspoon saffron threads

Heat the olive oil in a large heavy-based saucepan over medium–high heat and cook the ribs in batches until golden. Add the onion and cook for 5 minutes, or until softened. Stir in the tomato and paprika and cook for a few minutes more.

Add the pork sausages, chorizo and the stock (reserving 2 tablespoons) and bring to the boil. Reduce to a simmer and add the spaghettini. Cook, covered, for 15 minutes, or until the pasta is al dente.

Meanwhile, to make the picada, in a mortar and pestle or food processor, crush the nuts with the garlic, parsley, cinnamon and bread to make a paste. Stir in the saffron. If the mixture is too dry, add 1–2 tablespoons of the reserved stock. Stir into the casserole and simmer for 5 minutes, or until the casserole has thickened slightly. Season well before serving.

SERVES 4–6

Right: The spaghettini needs to be broken into pieces about half the length of your little finger.

Far right: Stir the picada through the noodles towards the end of cooking to thicken and add flavour.

Cocido Madrileño
Madrid Hotpot

A cocido can contain any type of meat to hand, plus chickpeas. The one constant, according to the old song, 'cocidito madrileño' (little stew from Madrid), is '… all the charm and the spice/that a woman's love puts right/into the cocidito madrileño'.

220 g (8 oz/1 cup) dried chickpeas
1 kg (2 lb 4 oz) chicken, trussed
500 g (1 lb 2 oz) beef brisket, in one piece
250 g (9 oz) piece smoke-cured bacon
125 g (5 oz) tocino, streaky bacon or speck
1 pig's trotter
200 g (7 oz) chorizo
1 brown onion, studded with 2 cloves
1 bay leaf
1 morcilla blood sausage (optional)

250 g (9 oz) green beans, trimmed and sliced
   lengthways
250 g (9 oz) green cabbage, cut into sections through
   the heart
300 g (11 oz) silverbeet (Swiss chard) leaves, washed
   well, stalks removed
8 small potatoes
3 leeks, white part only, cut into 10 cm (4 in) lengths
pinch of saffron threads
75 g (3 oz) dried rice vermicelli

Soak the dried chickpeas in cold water overnight. Drain and rinse, then tie them loosely in a muslin (cheesecloth) bag.

Put 3 litres (105 fl oz/12 cups) of cold water in a very large deep saucepan. Add the chicken, beef, bacon and tocino and bring to the boil. Add the chickpeas, pig's trotter and chorizo, return to the boil, then add the onion, bay leaf and ½ teaspoon salt. Simmer, partially covered, for 2½ hours (skim the surface occasionally if necessary) or until the meats are tender.

After 2 hours, bring a saucepan of water to the boil, add the morcilla (if using) and gently boil for 5 minutes. Drain and set aside. Loosely tie the beans in a muslin bag. Pour 1 litre (35 fl oz/4 cups) water into the saucepan and bring to the boil. Add the cabbage, silverbeet, potatoes, leek and saffron with 1 teaspoon salt. Return to the boil, then simmer for 30 minutes. Add the beans for the last 10 minutes of cooking.

Strain the stock from both the meat and vegetable pans and combine in a large saucepan. Bring to the boil, adjust the seasoning and stir in the vermicelli. Simmer for 6–7 minutes.

Release the chickpeas and pile them in the centre of a large warm platter. Discard the tocino, then slice the meats and sausages. Arrange in groups around the chickpeas at one end of the platter. Release the beans. Arrange the vegetables in groups around the other end. Spoon a little of the simmering broth (minus the vermicelli) over the meat, then pour the rest into a soup tureen, along with the vermicelli. Serve at once. It is traditional to serve both dishes together, although the broth is eaten first.

SERVES 6–8

BERENJENAS RELLENAS
Stuffed Eggplant

The eggplant, beloved of the Moors (the word 'berenjena' is of Moorish origin), was adopted enthusiastically by the Spanish. This dish is a classic of the medieval cuisine of the Moorish occupation. Simple, yet tasty, making the most of local produce.

2 eggplants (aubergines)
80 ml (3 fl oz/⅓ cup) extra virgin olive oil
200 g (7 oz) minced (ground) lamb
2 garlic cloves, crushed
1 tomato, chopped

1 red onion, finely diced
1 egg
¼ teaspoon ground cinnamon
1 slice of white bread, crust removed, soaked in milk
2 tablespoons chopped flat-leaf (Italian) parsley

Cut the eggplant in half lengthways across the diagonal. Carefully make slices across the eggplant, starting 1 cm (½ in) in from the outside skin, then slice the opposite way, making a diamond effect. Sprinkle with salt, and leave for 20 minutes.

Preheat the oven to 200°C (400°F/Gas 6). Cover a baking tray with foil and brush with some of the oil, then place the eggplant cut side down on the tray. Bake for 20 minutes, or until softened. Cool slightly, then use a large kitchen spoon to scoop out the centre, leaving about 1 cm (½ in) border of eggplant flesh near the skin. Discard half of the pulp, finely chop the other half and set aside.

Combine the lamb mince, garlic, tomato, onion, egg, cinnamon, soaked bread and parsley. Add the chopped eggplant and mix again. Season with salt and pepper.

Divide the lamb mixture among the eggplant shells. Place in a roasting tin and drizzle with the remaining olive oil. Bake for 40 minutes, or until the meat is cooked through.

SERVES 4

A large metal spoon is the best implement for scooping out the eggplant in one piece.

CALDERETA DE CORDERO
Lamb Caldereta

This stew is from the Huelva Dehesa, the sparse Mediterranean woodlands of the Huelva region. For hundreds of years the Iberian pigs and sheep have roamed here and this dish can be traced back to the traditional food of the shepherds of the region.

2 tablespoons olive oil
1 brown onion, roughly diced
1 carrot, roughly diced
1 red capsicum (pepper), cut into large dice
2 garlic cloves, chopped
1 kg (2 lb 4 oz) lamb leg, boned and cut into
    2 cm (³/4 in) cubes
1 ham bone or trimmings
400 g (14 oz) tinned chopped tomatoes

2 tablespoons chopped flat-leaf (Italian) parsley
2 tablespoons chopped mint
2 tablespoons tomato paste (concentrated purée)
2 bay leaves
250 ml (9 fl oz/1 cup) white wine
25 g (1 oz/¼ cup) dry breadcrumbs
1 teaspoon ground cumin
1 teaspoon sweet paprika (pimentón)
½ teaspoon ground cinnamon

Preheat the oven to 180°C (350°F/Gas 4). Heat the oil in a large flameproof casserole dish over medium heat and cook the onion, carrot, capsicum and garlic until softened, about 8 minutes. Add the lamb cubes, ham bone or trimmings, tomato, parsley, mint, tomato paste, bay leaves, white wine and 185 ml (6 fl oz/³/4 cup) water. Bring to the boil, then cover and bake for 1–1½ hours, or until the lamb is tender.

Meanwhile, combine the breadcrumbs, cumin, paprika, cinnamon and a pinch of pepper.

Remove the lamb from the casserole dish with a slotted spoon or tongs and set aside. Discard the bay leaves and ham bone. Purée the remaining liquid and vegetables, then stir in the breadcrumb mixture. Cook, stirring, for about 10 minutes, or until the sauce has thickened. Return the lamb to the casserole dish and gently warm through. Season to taste. Serve with green beans.

SERVES 4

Far left: Remove the cooked lamb from the casserole while you purée the vegetables.

Left: The breadcrumb mixture helps to thicken the stew.

Lentejas con Chorizo

Stewed Lentils with Chorizo

Lentils are a pulse widely used around the Mediterranean, in soups, stews and salads, although the Spanish don't often use them. However, they do team them with sweet and smoky chorizo and added pimentón, creating a simple hearty winter meal.

400 g (14 oz) green lentils
100 ml (4 fl oz) olive oil
2 garlic cloves, crushed
1 green capsicum (pepper), seeded and diced
2 brown onions, chopped
2 teaspoons sweet paprika (pimentón)

1 bay leaf
2 slices bacon, cut into thin strips
200 g (7 oz) chorizo, sliced
1 tomato, chopped
extra virgin olive oil, for drizzling

Rinse the lentils, then cover with cold water and soak for 2 hours.

Heat 1 tablespoon of the oil in a large saucepan over medium heat and cook the garlic, capsicum and half the onion for 5 minutes, or until the onion is softened. Add the drained lentils, paprika, bay leaf and most of the remaining oil. Cover with water, bring to the boil, then reduce the heat and simmer for 30 minutes, or until tender.

Meanwhile, heat the remaining oil in a frying pan over medium heat. Add the bacon, chorizo and remaining onion and fry for 10 minutes, or until golden. Add to the lentil mixture with the tomato and a large pinch of salt, and cook for a further 5 minutes. Drizzle a little extra virgin olive oil over the top and serve.

SERVES 4

Canalones a la Barcelonesa

Barcelona-style Cannelloni

Canalones, as they are known in Spain, are just one of the many types of pasta used in the area. This dish is typical of Barcelona, and is an adaptation of the original brought by Italian migrants who came to the city in the nineteenth century.

2 tablespoons olive oil
125 g (5 oz) minced (ground) beef
125 g (5 oz) minced (ground) pork
200 g (7 oz) chicken livers, chopped
1 brown onion, diced
1 leek, white part only, halved lengthways and chopped
2½ tablespoons fino sherry
1 tablespoon chopped thyme
400 g (14 oz) tinned chopped tomatoes

4 tablespoons chopped flat-leaf (Italian) parsley
75 g (3 oz) butter
60 g (2 oz/½ cup) plain (all-purpose) flour
1 litre (35 fl oz/4 cups) milk
pinch of ground nutmeg
250 g (9 oz) packet dried cannelloni tubes
100 ml (4 fl oz) tomato passata (puréed tomato)
100 g (4 oz/1 cup) grated Manchego or parmesan cheese

Preheat the oven to 180°C (350°F/Gas 4). Heat the olive oil in a large heavy-based frying pan over medium heat. Cook the beef, pork, chicken livers, onion and leek for 10 minutes, or until browned, breaking up any lumps with the back of a wooden spoon. Add the sherry, thyme, tomato and half the parsley and cook for 3 minutes, or until most of the liquid has evaporated. Season and leave to cool.

Melt the butter in a large saucepan over medium heat. Add the flour and cook, stirring with a wooden spoon, for 1–2 minutes, until pale yellow. Remove from the heat and add the milk gradually, stirring constantly until blended. Return to the heat and slowly bring the mixture to the boil, whisking for 15 minutes, or until thickened. Season with nutmeg, salt and pepper.

Fill the cannelloni with the meat mixture using a wide-tip piping (icing) bag or a spoon. Put the filled cannelloni side by side in a buttered ovenproof dish. Pour the white sauce over the top and dot with the puréed tomato. Top with the grated cheese and bake for 40–45 minutes. Garnish with the remaining chopped parsley.

SERVES 6

POLLO RELLENO
Stuffed Chicken

Until not so long ago, the chickens of Spain could be found pecking around under orange and olive trees, the open grazing working their muscles, flavouring their meat. To make this simple meal, be sure to use an organic or at least free-range chicken.

100 g (4 oz) ham or bacon, chopped
100 g (4 oz) minced (ground) pork
2 tablespoons chopped flat-leaf (Italian) parsley
1 garlic clove, crushed
pinch of ground nutmeg
½ red onion, finely diced

1 teaspoon finely chopped oregano
2 tablespoons lemon juice
1 egg, beaten
1.6 kg (3 lb 8 oz) chicken
2 tablespoons olive oil

Preheat the oven to 200°C (400°F/Gas 6). To make the stuffing, mix together the ham, pork, parsley, garlic, nutmeg, onion, oregano and lemon juice. Add the beaten egg and mix with your hands until thoroughly combined. Season well.

Wash and pat dry the chicken inside and out, then loosely fill the cavity with the stuffing. Tie the legs together and put the chicken in a roasting tin. Rub with the oil, season with salt and pepper and roast for 30 minutes.

Reduce the heat to 180°C (350°F/Gas 4) and cook for a further 35–40 minutes, or until the juices run clear when the chicken is pierced between the thigh and body. Allow the chicken to rest for 10–15 minutes before carving. Serve a little of the stuffing with each portion of chicken.

SERVES 4

Loosely pack the stuffing into the chicken cavity using very clean hands.

COCHIFRITO

Lamb Stew

What most Spanish people eat today is very much what the Spaniards have eaten for hundreds of years. A bowl of filling, tasty cochifrito, served on a winter's night in front of a warm fire with bread and a glass of local wine, is as appealing now as it ever was.

80 ml (3 fl oz/⅓ cup) olive oil
1 kg (2 lb 4 oz) lamb shoulder, diced
1 large brown onion, finely chopped
4 garlic cloves, crushed

2 teaspoons sweet paprika (pimentón)
100 ml (4 fl oz) lemon juice
2 tablespoons chopped flat-leaf (Italian) parsley

Heat the oil in a large, deep heavy-based frying pan over high heat and cook the lamb in two batches for 5 minutes each batch, or until well browned. Remove all the lamb from the pan.

Add the onion to the pan and cook for 5 minutes, or until soft and golden. Stir in the garlic and paprika and cook for 1 minute. Return the lamb to the pan and add 80 ml (3 fl oz/⅓ cup) of the lemon juice and 1.75 litres (61 fl oz/7 cups) water. Bring to the boil, then reduce the heat to a simmer and cook, stirring occasionally, for about 2 hours, or until the liquid has almost evaporated and the oil starts to reappear. Stir in the parsley and remaining lemon juice, season with salt and freshly ground black pepper, and serve.

PICTURE ON PAGE 166

SERVES 4–6

Right: Brown the lamb in two batches to prevent overcrowding the frying pan.

Far right: The flavours in this stew rely heavily on browning the onions well.

Lamb Stew (recipe on page 165)

Paella Valenciana de la Huerta
Valencian Paella

The original paella, as still made in Valencia, using vegetables from the market gardens and any animals that could be caught in the delta – rabbit and snail – or chicken. It is cooked, preferably, in a paellera, over charcoal, outdoors in the open air.

100 g (4 oz/½ cup) dried lima beans (butter beans)
100 g (4 oz) dried cannellini beans
100 ml (4 fl oz) olive oil
2 boneless chicken breasts, skin on, cut into quarters
2 rabbit legs and thighs, jointed
125 g (5 oz) green beans, cut into thirds

1 tomato, seeded and finely chopped (see page 246)
large pinch of saffron threads
1 tablespoon sweet paprika (pimentón)
2 litres (70 fl oz/8 cups) chicken stock
sprig of rosemary
350 g (12 oz) Spanish rice (La Bomba or Calaspara)

Soak the lima and cannellini beans overnight in lots of cold water, then drain and rinse.

Heat the oil over medium–high heat in a 40 cm (16 in) paellera (or a heavy frying pan) with a little salt. Cook the chicken and rabbit in batches for 4–5 minutes, or until golden brown. Return all of the chicken and rabbit to the pan.

Reduce the heat to low, add the green beans and cook for a further 5 minutes. Add the tomato and fry for 3 minutes, or until thickened slightly.

Meanwhile, crush the saffron, then dissolve it in a little boiling water.

Stir the paprika into the paella, quickly add the stock and bring to the boil. Add the soaked beans and return to the boil. Add the rosemary sprig and saffron and simmer for 30 minutes for the flavours to develop and liquid to reduce slightly.

Increase the heat to high and sprinkle the rice into the pan. Bring to the boil and cook for 5 minutes, then gradually reduce the heat and simmer for 15 minutes, or until the liquid has evaporated and the rice is cooked. Season to taste.

If there is a small, almost burnt, crusty spot on the bottom centre of the paellera or frying pan, that's the best bit – give it to a favoured guest.

SERVES 4

Right: Brown the chicken and rabbit pieces in batches until golden brown.

Far right: Sprinkle the rice into the pan and bring to the boil before simmering until tender.

PATO CON PERAS

Duck with Pears

This Catalan favourite would most likely be made using the duck farmed in the Ampurdán region, the barbary, or muscovy, duck, which are large and have rich-tasting meat. For best results, use amontillado sherry and very firm, ripe pears.

¼ teaspoon ground nutmeg
½ teaspoon smoked paprika (pimentón)
pinch of ground cloves
2 kg (4 lb 8 oz) duck, jointed into 8 pieces
1 tablespoon olive oil
1 bay leaf
8 French shallots, peeled
8 baby carrots, trimmed
2 garlic cloves, sliced

80 ml (3 fl oz/⅓ cup) rich sweet sherry such
  as amontillado
1 thyme sprig
1 cinnamon stick
1 litre (35 fl oz/4 cups) chicken stock
4 firm ripe pears, peeled, halved and cored
60 g (2 oz) whole almonds, toasted
25 g (1 oz) dark bittersweet chocolate, grated

Preheat the oven to 180°C (350°F/Gas 4). In a small bowl, mix together the nutmeg, paprika, cloves and a little salt and pepper. Dust the duck pieces with the spice mixture. Heat the oil in a large flameproof casserole dish and, when hot, brown the duck in batches. Remove from the dish.

Drain off all but 1 tablespoon of fat from the dish. Add the bay leaf, shallots and carrots. Cook over medium heat for 3–4 minutes, or until lightly browned. Stir in the garlic and cook for 1 minute. Pour in the sherry and boil for 1 minute to deglaze the casserole dish. Stir in the thyme, cinnamon stick and stock. Return the duck to the dish.

Bring to the boil, then transfer the casserole to the oven and bake, covered, for 1 hour 10 minutes, turning the duck halfway through. Put the pears on top of the duck and bake for another 20 minutes.

Meanwhile, finely grind the almonds in a food processor, then combine with the chocolate.

When the duck is cooked, lift the duck pieces and the pears out of the liquid using a slotted spoon and transfer to a serving dish with the carrots, shallots and cinnamon stick. Keep warm.

Put the casserole dish on the stovetop and bring the liquid to the boil over medium heat. Boil for 7–10 minutes, or until reduced by half. Add 60 ml (2 fl oz/¼ cup) of the hot liquid to the almonds and chocolate and stir to combine. Whisk the paste into the rest of the sauce to thicken. Season to taste, pour over the duck and serve.

SERVES 4

ANDRAJOS CON BACALAO

Tatters and Rags

The name of this Andalucían dish probably refers to original recipes which included flour and water for making little square dumplings (the rags and tatters). The same effect is created in this modern take on a classic by using lasagne sheets.

500 g (1 lb 2 oz) bacalao (salt cod)
2 tablespoons olive oil
1 onion, chopped
2 garlic cloves, finely chopped
400 g (14 oz) tinned chopped tomatoes
½ teaspoon sweet paprika (pimentón)
½ teaspoon smoked paprika (pimentón)
pinch of saffron threads

10 black peppercorns
1 teaspoon cumin seeds
500 ml (17 fl oz/2 cups) chicken stock
100 g (4 oz) dried lasagne sheets, cut in half to form squares approximately 9 x 9 cm (3½ x 3½ in)
2 tablespoons chopped flat-leaf (Italian) parsley
1 tablespoon lemon juice

Soak the bacalao in plenty of cold water for about 20 hours in the fridge, changing the water four or five times to remove excess saltiness.

Drain the bacalao, then put it in a large saucepan and cover with cold water. Bring to the boil, then reduce the heat and simmer for 20 minutes, or until the fish is soft and able to be removed from the bone. Drain the bacalo and set aside until cool, then shred.

Heat the oil in a large, heavy-based flameproof casserole dish over medium heat. Cook the onion and garlic for about 5 minutes, or until softened.

Add the chopped tomato and cook for 2 minutes. Stir in the sweet and smoked paprika and the shredded fish.

Using a mortar and pestle or food processor, grind the saffron threads, peppercorns and cumin seeds to a powder. Add to the casserole with the chicken stock and simmer for 15 minutes, or until reduced to a sauce consistency.

Meanwhile, cook the lasagne sheets in boiling water until al dente. Stir into the casserole and season to taste. Garnish with the parsley, drizzle the lemon juice over the top and serve.

SERVES 4

CHEESE

Over three days every year, at the end of April, cheeses of Spain, from the lush Queso de la Serena to the wild blue Cabrales, are celebrated at the Trujillo Cheese Fair held in the main plaza of the ancient and beautiful hilltop town overlooking the plains of Extremadura in western Spain.

Over 100,000 people descend on the fair, revelling in Spain's best cheeses. It is the ideal way to try them all, since tracking down all the cheeses on show would take you from the blue cheese centres in the Picos de Europa down through to Extremadura, home to luscious sheep milk cheese of Torta de la Serena and Torta de Casar; to Zamora for the sharp Zamorano sheep milk cheeses; across to Cantabria for the buttery Queso de Cantabria and tart cow milk cheeses of Liebana; to Catalonia for goat milk Garrotxa; to La Mancha for the famous Manchego; and by ferry to Menorca for creamy Mahon.

Even then, you will only have seen a fraction of it. New cheeses are being added to the list every day.

A visit to the weekly market at Cangas de Onis in the province of Asturias will yield, in addition to the traditional cheeses of the region, like the Gamoneu (the smallest Denominación de Origen (D.O.) cheese in Spain), a remarkable number made by cheese makers who have no allegiance to a particular D.O. or tradition: they just love making cheese.

The making of cheese, like all the Spanish artisanal products, has moved into the twenty-first century. While the cheeses are still made by hand, biologists have joined traditional cheese makers in teaching new generations the craft.

Using cow, goat and sheep milk, Spanish cheese producers make the most of the diverse range of climates, creating over 100 official cheeses with 12 of them protected by the D.O. Some types of cheese, goat's milk cheese for example, are stored in jars with olive oil and herbs.

As with the tradition of grazing sheep across the countryside between milkings, Spain prides itself on maintaining many of its traditional production processes. Although the cheese industry processes have been modernized, many prefer to adhere to time-honoured methods.

Just as Spanish wine is conquering the world, Spanish cheese is now claiming its place on the world's cheeseboards.

SIERRA DE CADIZ
CABRA LECHE
CRUDA
1200 EUROS
KILO

Puro de
CABRA
0 EUROS
KILO

ANCHOAS
OLIVA
1€

ANCHOAS

PICANTE
Queso Curado
de Cabra
13'00 EUROS
KILO

GUISADO DE POLLO AL AZAFRÁN
Chicken in Saffron Stew

This dish is typical to the Castilla – La Mancha area, in the centre of the Iberian Peninsula. Characteristic of the local cuisine, this dish is flavoured with saffron and thickened and enriched with almonds and egg yolks.

60 ml (2 fl oz/¼ cup) olive oil
50 g (2 oz/⅓ cup) blanched almonds
1 thick slice bread, crusts removed, cut into pieces
½ teaspoon ground cinnamon
pinch of saffron threads
2 garlic cloves
2 tablespoons chopped flat-leaf (Italian) parsley
1.5 kg (3 lb 5 oz) chicken, cut into 8 pieces
  and seasoned with salt

2 brown onions, finely chopped
125 ml (4 fl oz/½ cup) fino sherry
375 ml (13 fl oz/1½ cups) chicken stock
1 bay leaf
2 thyme sprigs
2 tablespoons lemon juice
2 egg yolks

Heat 1 tablespoon of the olive oil in a heavy-based flameproof casserole dish over medium–high heat. Add the blanched almonds and bread and fry for 3 minutes, or until golden. Remove and drain on paper towel. When cooled slightly, put in a mortar and pestle or food processor, add the cinnamon, saffron, garlic and half the parsley, and grind or process to a coarse, crumbly consistency.

Heat the remaining oil in the casserole dish over medium heat and brown the chicken pieces for about 5 minutes. Transfer the chicken to a plate. Add the onion to the casserole dish and cook gently for 5 minutes, or until softened.

Return the chicken pieces to the casserole dish with the sherry, chicken stock, bay leaf and thyme and simmer, covered, over medium heat for 1 hour, or until the chicken is tender. Remove the chicken and cover to keep warm. Add the almond paste to the dish and cook for 1 minute. Remove from the heat and whisk in the lemon juice, egg yolks and remaining parsley.

Return the casserole dish to the stovetop and stir over very low heat until just thickened slightly (do not allow it to boil or the sauce will separate). Season to taste, return the chicken to the casserole and gently warm through before serving.

SERVES 4

Guisado de Cerdo Estofado con Legumbres
Spanish Pork and Vegetable Stew

Perfect on a wintery night with a big glass of rioja, this rustic and comforting stew is a variation on the style popular in central Spain. Using delicious products local to the area, it is packed full of flavour: smoky chorizo, sweet capsicums and rich tomatoes.

600 g (1 lb 5 oz) boneless pork shoulder (hand/collar butt)
4 (100 g/4 oz each) all-purpose potatoes, peeled
1 red capsicum (pepper)
1 green capsicum (pepper)
2 tablespoons olive oil
1 large red onion, chopped
2 garlic cloves, crushed

100 g (4 oz) jamón
1 chorizo, sliced
2 x 400 g (14 oz) tins tomatoes, chopped
½ bunch thyme
2 tablespoons sherry vinegar
100 ml (4 fl oz) white wine
1 bay leaf
250 ml (9 fl oz/1 cup) chicken stock

Cut the pork into 2.5 cm (1 in) pieces. Peel the potatoes and cut them into pieces the same size as the pork. Chop the capsicums into 2.5 cm (1 in) squares, removing the seeds and white membrane.

Preheat the oven to 180°C (350°F/Gas 4). Place a large frying pan over medium heat. Heat the oil, then add the pork, onions and garlic. Cook for 5 minutes, or until the onion is softened and the

meat is lightly browned all over. Next add the capsicums, jamón and chorizo. Continue to cook, stirring occasionally, for another 5 minutes, or until the liquid is slightly reduced.

Transfer the mixture to a large, deep casserole dish. Add the remaining ingredients and season with salt and pepper. Place in the oven and cook for 2 hours, or until the meat is very tender.

SERVES 4–6

When the liquid has reduced slightly, transfer the stew to an ovenproof cooking vessel.

Arroz Rosetxat

Valencian Lamb and Rice

A traditional meal, originally designed to use up the left-over meat and broth from a cocido (a stew usually comprised of meat and chickpeas, see page 152) and finished in the oven – another Spanish dish proving there's more to rice than paella.

100 g (4 oz/½ cup) chickpeas
1 red onion
1 parsnip
1 celery stalk
1 turnip
200 g (7 oz) diced lamb leg
1 pig's ear, about 150–200 g (6–7 oz), salted if possible
100 g (4 oz) minced (ground) pork
4 tablespoons fine fresh breadcrumbs

50 g (2 oz) jamón, finely chopped
1 egg
pinch of ground cinnamon
3 tablespoons chopped flat-leaf (Italian) parsley
1 morcilla or other blood sausage, about 200 g (7 oz)
1 white catalan sausage, butifarra or other mild pork sausage, about 200 g (7 oz)
2 tablespoons olive oil
1 garlic clove, finely chopped
300 g (11 oz/1⅓ cups) short-grain rice

Soak the dried chickpeas in water for 3–4 hours, then drain.

Meanwhile, chop the onion, parsnip, celery and turnip into 2 cm (¾ in) dice and set aside. Bring 2 litres (70 fl oz/8 cups) of water to the boil in a large saucepan. Add the lamb and whole pig's ear. Bring the water back to the boil, then reduce to a steady simmer and cook for 30 minutes. Add the drained chickpeas, diced onion, parsnip, celery and turnip and season to taste – if the pig's ear was salted you may not need any more salt. Continue to simmer for another 20 minutes.

Meanwhile, combine the pork mince with the fresh breadcrumbs, jamón, egg, cinnamon and 1 tablespoon of the chopped parsley. Season well. Take heaped teaspoons of the mixture and roll it into balls.

Add the whole sausages and the meatballs to the pan. Return to a simmer and cook for 10 minutes, or until the meatballs are firm to the touch and cooked through. Cover and turn off the heat.

Preheat the oven to 180°C (350°F/Gas 4). Place a heavy-based flameproof casserole on the stovetop over medium–high heat. Add the olive oil and garlic and cook, stirring, for 2 minutes, or until the garlic is lightly golden. Add the rice and stir for another minute. Stir in 600 ml (21 fl oz) of the cooking liquid from the stew. Bring to the boil, cover and bake for 20 minutes, or until the rice is cooked. Gently reheat the stew and serve with the rice, garnished with the remaining parsley.

SERVES 4–6

POLLO A LA CERVEZA

Chicken in Beer

The use of beer in this popular dish gives it a unique, stew-like consistency. A tasty, flavoursome dish, pollo a la cerveza is a common weeknight meal for many Spanish families and is fine for kids as the alcohol content is eliminated during cooking.

350 ml (12 fl oz) bottle of beer (Spanish if possible)
1 tablespoon dijon mustard
1 teaspoon sweet paprika (pimentón)
2 brown onions, diced
2 garlic cloves, crushed
1.5 kg (2 lb 12 oz) chicken, cut into pieces

2 tablespoons olive oil
1 green capsicum (pepper), diced
400 g (14 oz) tinned chopped tomatoes
1 onion, extra, diced
1 garlic clove, extra, crushed

Combine the beer, dijon mustard, paprika, half the onion, half the garlic and a large pinch of salt in a large bowl. Add the chicken pieces and toss until well coated. Cover and marinate overnight in the refrigerator.

Preheat the oven to 180°C (350°F/Gas 4). Heat the olive oil in a large flameproof casserole dish over medium heat. Add the diced capsicum and the remaining onion and garlic and cook for 10 minutes, or until softened.

Stir in the chicken, marinade and tomato and season well. Cover and bake for 45–60 minutes, or until the chicken is tender.

SERVES 4

Overnight refrigeration helps the flavour to permeate and to tenderize the chicken.

Venison con Jerez y Cabrales

Venison in Sherry with Cabrales Cheese

Modern Spanish cooks are taking advantage of the country's array of wonderful cheeses and defying a tradition that rarely cooked with them. This recipe is typical of such inventions and a truly lovely dish.

1 kg (2 lb 4 oz) venison leg meat, cut into 2.5 cm
  (1 in) cubes
250 ml (9 fl oz/1 cup) Pedro Ximénez (or other rich
  sweet Spanish sherry)
1 leek, white part only
1 carrot
1 celery stalk
1 red onion
2 tablespoons olive oil

12 garlic cloves, roughly chopped
100 g (4 oz) jamón, diced
2 tablespoons tomato paste (concentrated purée)
250 ml (9 fl oz/1 cup) beef stock
a few sprigs thyme, chopped
2 tablespoons chopped marjoram
100 g (4 oz) cabrales cheese (or roquefort)
3 tablespoons cream
1 tablespoon Pedro Ximénez sherry, extra

Place the venison in a bowl, pour over the sherry and toss to combine. Cover and marinate in the refrigerator for 24 hours, stirring occasionally.

Preheat the oven to 180°C (350°F/Gas 4). Drain the venison, reserving the marinade. Cut the leek, carrot, celery and onion into 1 cm (½ in) dice.

Put the olive oil in a heavy-based flameproof casserole over medium heat. Add the vegetables, garlic and jamón. Cook, stirring, for 5 minutes, or until softened. Increase the heat to medium–high, add the venison and stir for about 2 minutes, or until sealed and light brown in colour.

Add the reserved marinade, tomato paste, beef stock and herbs. Cover and place in the oven for 2 hours, stirring occasionally, until the venison is tender and the sauce reduced and thickened.

Meanwhile, put the cabrales cheese in a bowl with 1 tablespoon of the cream and mash together well. Combine the remaining cream and sherry in a small saucepan over low heat. When warm, stir in the cheese until melted and smooth.

Remove the venison from the oven and serve drizzled with the cheese mixture.

PICTURE ON PAGE 186

SERVES 4

Venison in Sherry with Cabrales Cheese (recipe on page 185)

Beato Marcelo Spínola
Retablo donado por El Correo
De Andalucía a la Hermandad
Sacramental de la Soledad

Guisado Gitano

Gypsy Stew

The gitanos, gypsies, have been an important part of Spain's cultural life for hundreds of years. There are various dishes like this one, traditionally called olla gitana. Why they are named after them is a mystery. No matter, just enjoy; they are all delicious.

250 g (9 oz/1¼ cups) dried white haricot beans
  (such as navy beans)
80 ml (3 fl oz/⅓ cup) olive oil
2 garlic cloves, chopped
2 brown onions, chopped
1 teaspoon sweet paprika (pimentón)
1 teaspoon smoked paprika (pimentón)
2 teaspoons ground cumin
¼ teaspoon ground cinnamon
¼ teaspoon cayenne pepper

1 teaspoon dried rosemary
1 red capsicum (pepper), seeded and diced
750 g (1 lb 10 oz) pork tenderloin, roughly diced
400 g (14 oz) tinned chopped tomatoes
250 ml (9 fl oz/1 cup) chicken stock
300 g (11 oz) orange sweet potato, peeled and
  roughly diced
60 g (2 oz) silverbeet (Swiss chard), washed well
  and shredded

Cover the beans with cold water and soak for at least 3 hours. Drain well.

Preheat the oven to 160°C (315°F/Gas 2–3). Heat 2 tablespoons of the oil in a large saucepan over medium heat, add half the garlic and half the onion and cook for 5 minutes, or until soft. Add the beans and cover with water. Bring to the boil, then reduce the heat and simmer for 45 minutes, or until the beans are soft but not mushy.

Meanwhile, heat the remaining olive oil in a large flameproof casserole dish over medium heat. Add the remaining chopped garlic and onion and cook

for 5 minutes, or until softened. Stir in the spices, rosemary, capsicum and diced pork and cook until the pork is pale brown. Add the tomato and stock, bring to the boil, then cover and cook in the oven for 1 hour.

Add the beans and diced sweet potato, top up with 250 ml (9 fl oz/1 cup) water and return to the oven for 30 minutes, or until the sweet potato is tender. Stir in the silverbeet and cook for 5 minutes, or until the silverbeet is wilted. Season to taste.

SERVES 4

Conejo en Vino Tinto
Rabbit in Red Wine

Two ingredients beloved of the Spanish: the rabbit, which would often be from the home hutch; and red wine, always loved and today, with improved techniques, often wonderful. Use the same wine in the recipe as you intend to drink with the meal.

2 x 1 kg (2 lb 4 oz) rabbits, jointed and cut into
   8 pieces each
100 ml (4 fl oz) olive oil
1 large brown onion, chopped
6 roma (plum) tomatoes, peeled and chopped
   (see page 246)
1 teaspoon sweet paprika (pimentón)
6 garlic cloves, crushed

3 slices jamón or prosciutto, cut into strips
100 g (4 oz) chorizo, chopped
3 red capsicums (peppers), seeded and diced
   (see page 246)
2 tablespoons chopped thyme
250 ml (9 fl oz/1 cup) red wine
1 handful flat-leaf (Italian) parsley, chopped

Season the rabbit pieces. Heat half the oil in a heavy-based flameproof casserole over medium heat and cook the rabbit in batches for about 4 minutes per batch, or until golden brown. Remove and set aside.

Heat the rest of the oil in the dish and cook the onion for 5 minutes, or until softened. Add the tomato and simmer gently for 10 minutes. Stir in the paprika, garlic, jamón, chorizo, capsicum, thyme, red wine, rabbit pieces and 2 tablespoons of the parsley. Check the seasoning. Bring to the boil, then reduce the heat and simmer for 35 minutes, or until the rabbit is tender.

Remove the rabbit pieces and simmer the sauce for 20–30 minutes, or until reduced and slightly thickened. Return the rabbit to the casserole and gently heat through. Season to taste, garnish with the remaining parsley and serve.

SERVES 4

Set aside the rabbit pieces while you simmer the sauce until slightly thickened.

PERDICES CON COL A LA CATALANA
Catalan-style Partridge with Cabbage

This adaptation of the Catalan classic, perdices con col, roasted partridge with cabbage dumplings celebrates the Catalan love of hunting game and the Catalans' preference for earthy, gutsy simple flavours. Well worth the trouble.

2 partridges, about 400–500 g (14 oz–1 lb 2 oz) each
¼ teaspoon ground cinnamon
¼ teaspoon ground nutmeg
20 g (1 oz) butter
80 ml (3 fl oz/⅓ cup) olive oil
100 g (4 oz) jamón, diced
1 small red onion, finely diced
1 leek, white part only, finely diced
1 carrot, finely diced
1 tomato, seeded, diced
250 ml (9 fl oz/1 cup) white wine

250 ml (9 fl oz/1 cup) chicken stock
½ bunch thyme
1 bay leaf
150 g (6 oz) butifarra sausage (available from some Spanish delicatessens or butchers)
½ green cabbage
1 egg, lightly beaten
125 g (5 oz/1 cup) plain (all-purpose) flour
1 tablespoon pine nuts, lightly roasted
2 tablespoons flat-leaf (Italian) parsley
1 garlic clove

Preheat the oven to 180°C (350°F/Gas 4). Halve the partridges lengthways. Combine the ground cinnamon, nutmeg and 1 teaspoon salt and rub over the partridge pieces.

Heat the butter and 1 tablespoon of the oil in a heavy-based flameproof casserole over medium heat. Brown the partridges on all sides, for about 5 minutes, then remove.

Add the diced jamón, onion, leek and carrot to the casserole. Sauté until tender, about 5 minutes. Add the diced tomato, wine, stock, thyme, bay leaf and whole sausage, and return the partridge halves. Bring to the boil, then cover and transfer the dish to the oven. Cook for about 50–60 minutes, or until the birds are tender.

Meanwhile, bring a large saucepan of water to the boil. Cut out the cabbage core, then blanch the cabbage in the pan for 5 minutes. Remove each leaf and refresh in cold water. Drain well.

Remove the partridges and sausage from the casserole to cool. Slice the sausage and return it to the casserole.

Whisk the egg with 2 tablespoons of water in a shallow bowl. Put the flour in a shallow bowl. Remove the partridge meat from the bones. Wrap the meat in the cabbage leaves, making small parcels. Dip each parcel in the egg mixture, then in the flour.

Heat the remaining oil in a frying pan over medium heat. Fry each parcel for 3 minutes, or until lightly golden. Return the parcels to the casserole and bake for 20 minutes, or until hot.

Meanwhile, combine the pine nuts, parsley and garlic using a mortar and pestle to form a paste, or a picada. Remove the casserole from the oven. Remove the parcels. Stir the picada through the sauce and serve with the parcels.

SERVES 4

CORDONICES EN HOJAS DE PARRA

Quails in Vine Leaves

A wide variety of birds are used in Spanish cooking, from well-fed farm chickens to wild pheasants and even partridges, which are often served with a rich chocolate sauce. Quails, with their delicate-tasting flesh, are generally treated more simply.

8 quails
2 lemons, cut into quarters
8 slices jamón or prosciutto
16 vine leaves in brine, rinsed in cold water

1 tablespoon olive oil
60 ml (2 fl oz/¼ cup) veal or chicken stock
100 ml (4 fl oz) sweet sherry, such as oloroso
50 g (2 oz) chilled butter, diced

Preheat the oven to 200°C (400°F/Gas 6). Wash the quails and pat dry with paper towel. Put one lemon quarter inside each quail. Season and wrap each quail with a slice of jamón. Put a quail on top of two overlapping vine leaves, fold the leaves around the bird and secure with kitchen twine. Repeat with the remaining quails and leaves.

Put the wrapped quails in a roasting tin, drizzle with the oil and bake for 30 minutes. Remove from the oven and pierce one bird between the thigh and body through to the bone and check that the juices run out clear. If they are pink, cook for another 5 minutes. Transfer the quails to a separate plate to rest for 10 minutes, removing the twine and vine leaves.

Pour the remaining juices in the roasting tin into a small saucepan and add the stock and sherry. Bring to the boil and gradually whisk in the butter for 3 minutes, or until the sauce is slightly glazy. Serve the quail drizzled with the sauce.

SERVES 4

Right: Wrap the quails in the jamón and vine leaves.

Far right: Truss the wrapped quails with kitchen string to help hold their shape.

Fabada Asturiana

Asturian Stew

A dish made for men and women who were accustomed to bounding up mountains daily! It is properly made with Asturian faba beans (use them if you can). This tasty stew is eaten for lunch, after which you should go for a brisk walk. A winter wonder.

400 g (14 oz/2 cups) dried white haricot beans
  (such as navy beans)
700 g (1 lb 9 oz) smoked ham hock
2 tablespoons olive oil
150 g (6 oz) bacon, chopped
1 brown onion, chopped

2 garlic cloves, chopped
pinch of saffron threads
1 teaspoon sweet paprika (pimentón)
1 bay leaf
200 g (7 oz) morcilla blood sausages, sliced

Rinse the beans and soak overnight in cold water.

Put the ham hock in a large saucepan and cover with water. Bring to the boil, then reduce the heat and simmer for at least 1 hour, or until the meat is tender and starting to come away from the bone. Allow to cool, then remove the meat from the bone and cut it into large cubes. Reserve 1 litre (35 fl oz/4 cups) of the cooking liquid.

Heat the oil in a large heavy-based saucepan and cook the bacon, onion and garlic for 5 minutes,

or until translucent. Add the beans, cubed ham, saffron, paprika and bay leaf, and season to taste.

Add the reserved cooking liquid and bring to the boil, then reduce the heat and simmer for at least 1 hour, or until the beans are cooked (they should be soft but not mushy). Add the morcilla and cook for 5 minutes, or until heated through. Season before serving.

SERVES 4

When the ham hock is cool, pull the meat off the bone and cut it into cubes.

POLLO EN SAMFAINA

Chicken in Samfaina Sauce

Everyone else in Spain describes samfaina as the Catalan ratatouille, while the Catalans say that ratatouille is the Provençal samfaina. Either way, it works wonders with poultry, as here in this modern dish with fried chicken.

1.5 kg (3 lb 5 oz) chicken, cut into 8 pieces
60 ml (2 fl oz/¼ cup) olive oil
2 large brown onions, chopped
400 g (14 oz) eggplant (aubergine), peeled and cut
   into 2.5 cm (1 in) cubes
3 garlic cloves, crushed
350 g (12 oz) zucchini (courgettes), cut into strips

2 green or red capsicums (peppers), cut into 1 cm
   (½ in) strips
2 x 400 g (14 oz) tins chopped tomatoes
1 bay leaf
2 tablespoons chopped herbs (such as thyme, oregano
   and flat-leaf (Italian) parsley)
125 ml (4 fl oz/½ cup) white wine

Season the chicken pieces with salt and pepper. Heat the oil in a large heavy-based saucepan over medium heat, add the chicken pieces in batches and brown well all over. Remove from the pan and reduce the heat to low–medium.

Add the onion and cook for about 10 minutes, or until softened. Add the eggplant, garlic, zucchini and capsicum and cook for 10 minutes, or until the vegetables are softened.

Stir in the tomato, bay leaf, herbs and wine, and return the chicken pieces to the pan. Bring to the boil, then cover and simmer over low heat for about 45 minutes, or until the chicken is tender and the eggplant is soft. Season well with salt and pepper before serving.

SERVES 4

PIERNA DE CORDERO ASADO
Roast Leg of Lamb

The wood-fired oven-roasted lamb of the cities of Burgos and Segovia in Castile and León is famed across Spain for its flavour and tenderness – the waiter will carve it with the aid of a plate. Perfect with a glass of rich tempranillo from la Rioja.

1.5 kg (3 lb 5 oz) lamb leg
2 tablespoons olive oil
250 ml (9 fl oz/1 cup) white wine
150 g (6 oz/1 bunch) flat-leaf (Italian) parsley, chopped

2 teaspoons finely chopped rosemary
2 teaspoons finely chopped thyme
8 garlic cloves, crushed

Preheat the oven to 200°C (400°F/Gas 6). Rinse the lamb leg and pat dry with paper towel. Put the lamb in a roasting tin and drizzle the olive oil and wine over the top. Mix together the parsley, rosemary, thyme and garlic and sprinkle over the lamb, pressing down firmly.

Put the lamb in the oven and cook for 20 minutes, basting with the juices in the tin. Reduce the temperature to 180°C (350°F/Gas 4) and cook

for 1 hour. Remove from the oven and rest for at least 10 minutes before serving. The lamb will be medium–rare to medium. If you prefer your lamb a little less pink, cook for a further 5–10 minutes before resting.

SERVES 4

Press the mixed herbs and garlic into the top of the lamb to help them adhere.

Chapter 4

DESSERTS AND SWEETS

It is the Spanish way to start the day, and end the night, with delectable treats. Every region offers its own gift to satisfy the famed Spanish sweet tooth.

POLVORONES

Almond Shortbread

This dish takes its name from the word polvo, meaning powder – very fragile, they burst delightfully in the mouth as you eat them. Polvorones are a Spanish sweet that comes into its own as a treat for Christmas or Easter.

250 g (9 oz/2 cups) plain (all-purpose) flour, sifted
½ teaspoon ground aniseed
125 g (4½ oz/1 cup) icing (confectioners') sugar, sifted
250 g (9 oz) softened unsalted butter

1 egg yolk
1 teaspoon lemon juice
2 teaspoons fino (dry) sherry

In a large bowl, combine the sifted flour, aniseed, 1 tablespoon of icing sugar and a pinch of salt.

Beat the softened butter with electric beaters until pale and creamy, then beat in the egg yolk, lemon juice and sherry until well combined. Beat in half the flour mixture with the electric beaters, then stir in the remaining flour with a wooden spoon. Gather the dough into a ball with your hands, cover with plastic wrap and refrigerate for 1 hour.

Preheat the oven to 150°C (300°F/Gas 2). Roll out the chilled dough on a floured surface to a 1 cm (½ in) thickness. Using a 5 cm (2 in) cutter, cut into cookies (biscuits). Bake on an ungreased baking tray for 20 minutes, or until the biscuits are light brown and firm. Allow to cool slightly, then roll the biscuits in the remaining icing sugar. Cool completely, then roll in the icing sugar again. Store the biscuits, covered with any remaining sugar, for up to two weeks in an airtight container.

MAKES 20

Far left: Stamp out the cookies with a cutter.

Left: Roll the cookies in the icing sugar twice for a luscious powdery coating.

Chocolate con Churros

Churros and Hot Chocolate

A Spaniard would be puzzled by the inclusion of this recipe in a cookbook – they have only to walk to any corner café to be able to indulge in this extremely rich breakfast or late-night snack. For those of us who are not so lucky, here it is.

110 g (3³⁄₄ oz/¹⁄₂ cup) sugar
1 teaspoon ground cinnamon
30 g (1 oz) butter
150 g (5¹⁄₂ oz/1¹⁄₄ cups) plain (all-purpose) flour
¹⁄₂ teaspoon finely grated orange zest
¹⁄₄ teaspoon caster (superfine) sugar
2 eggs
vegetable or mild olive oil, for deep-frying

HOT CHOCOLATE
2 tablespoons cornflour (cornstarch)
1 litre (35 fl oz/4 cups) milk, plus 2 tablespoons, extra
200 g (7 oz) good-quality dark chocolate, chopped
sugar, to taste

Combine the sugar and cinnamon and spread the mixture out on a plate.

Put the butter, flour, orange zest, caster sugar, 170 ml (5¹⁄₂ fl oz/²⁄₃ cup) water and a pinch of salt in a heavy-based saucepan. Stir over low heat until the butter softens and the mixture forms a dough. Cook for 2–3 minutes, stirring constantly, until the dough forms a ball around the spoon and leaves a coating on the base of the pan.

Transfer the warm dough to a food processor and, with the motor running, add the eggs. Do not overprocess. If the dough is too soft to snip with scissors, return it to the pan and cook, stirring, over low heat until it is firmer. Spoon the dough into a piping bag fitted with a 5 mm (¹⁄₄ in) star nozzle.

Heat the oil in a wide saucepan to 180°C (350°F), or until a cube of bread dropped in the oil browns in 15 seconds. Pipe lengths of the batter 6–8 cm (2¹⁄₂–3¹⁄₄ in) long into the oil, a few at a time. An easy technique is to pipe with one hand and cut the batter off using kitchen scissors in the other hand. Cook the churros, turning once or twice, for about 3 minutes, or until puffed and golden. Drain each batch on paper towel. While still hot, toss the churros in the sugar mixture and serve at once.

To make the hot chocolate, mix the cornflour and 2 tablespoons of milk to a smooth paste. Put the chocolate and remaining milk in a saucepan and whisk constantly over low heat until just warm. Stir 2 tablespoons of the chocolate milk into the cornflour paste, then return all the paste to the milk. Whisking constantly, cook the mixture until it just begins to boil. Remove from the heat, add sugar to taste, and whisk for another minute. Serve with the hot churros.

SERVES 4

Bizcocho de Limón
Lemon Sponge Cake

Some recipes are almost universal, and in Spain, this sponge made with lemon is a basis for many desserts. It is delicious iced with lemon icing, and split and filled with lemon cream. Or simply serve with cream.

6 eggs, at room temperature
380 g (13 oz/1²/₃ cups) caster (superfine) sugar

2 teaspoons grated lemon zest
185 g (6½ oz/1½ cups) plain (all-purpose) flour, sifted

Preheat the oven to 160°C (315°F/Gas 2–3). Lightly grease and line a 24 cm (9½ in) spring-form tin.

Using electric beaters, beat the eggs and sugar for 15 minutes, or until light and creamy. Beat in the lemon zest. Using a large metal spoon or spatula, gently fold the flour into the egg mixture.

Pour the batter into the prepared tin and bake for 1 hour 10 minutes. Turn off the oven and leave the oven door open for 5 minutes. Remove the cake from the oven and leave it to cool completely in the tin.

SERVES 8

Far left: The eggs and sugar need to be really light and creamy.

Left: Use a large metal spoon to fold the flour into the egg and sugar mixture.

CREMA CATALANA

Catalan Custard

Those unfamiliar with Catalan cuisine may look at this dish and say, 'but this is the French dessert called crème brûlée'. On the other hand, a Catalan will indignantly look at a crème brûlée, and say, 'they've stolen our crema Catalana'.

1 litre (35 fl oz/4 cups) milk
1 vanilla bean, split
1 cinnamon stick
zest of 1 small lemon, cut into strips
2 strips orange zest, 4 x 2 cm (1½ x ¾ in)

8 egg yolks
115 g (4 oz/½ cup) caster (superfine) sugar
40 g (1½ oz/⅓ cup) cornflour (cornstarch)
45 g (1½ oz/¼ cup) soft brown sugar

Put the milk, scraped vanilla bean, cinnamon stick and lemon and orange zests in a saucepan and bring to the boil. Reduce the heat and simmer for 5 minutes, then strain and set aside.

Whisk the egg yolks with the caster sugar in a bowl for 5 minutes, or until pale and creamy. Add the cornflour and mix well. Slowly add the warm strained milk to the egg mixture while you whisk continuously. Return to the saucepan and cook over low–medium heat, stirring constantly, for 5–10 minutes, or until the mixture is thick and creamy. Do not allow it to boil as it will curdle. Pour into six 185 ml (6 fl oz/¾ cup) ramekins and refrigerate for 6 hours, or overnight.

When ready to serve, sprinkle the top of the custard evenly with brown sugar and grill (broil) for 3 minutes, or until it caramelizes.

SERVES 6

Far left: Scrape the vanilla seeds from the pod.

Left: Whisk the infused milk into the egg mixture, then stir until thick and creamy.

HIGOS RELLENOS

Stuffed Figs

The season for fresh figs is short and intense, but so abundant are the figs of Spain that they cannot all be eaten, so many are dried. Ingenious methods of utilizing these dried figs have been devised, including this sweet, syrupy offering.

175 g (6 oz/ ½ cup) honey
125 ml (4 fl oz/ ½ cup) oloroso sherry
¼ teaspoon ground cinnamon
18 large dried figs

18 whole blanched almonds
100 g (3½ oz) good-quality dark chocolate, cut into shards
thick (double/heavy) cream, for serving (optional)

Combine the honey, sherry, cinnamon and figs with 375 ml (13 fl oz/1½ cups) of water in a large saucepan over high heat. Bring to the boil, then reduce the heat and simmer for 10 minutes. Remove the pan from the heat and set aside for 3 hours. Remove the figs with a slotted spoon, reserving the liquid.

Preheat the oven to 180°C (350°F/Gas 4). Return the pan of liquid to the stove and boil over high heat for 5 minutes, or until syrupy, then set aside. Snip the stems from the figs with scissors, then cut

a slit in the top of each fig with a small sharp knife. Push an almond and a few shards of chocolate into each slit. Put the figs in a lightly buttered ovenproof dish and bake for 15 minutes, or until the chocolate has melted.

Serve three figs per person, with a little of the syrup and a dollop of cream.

PICTURE ON PAGE 214

SERVES 6

Stuff the figs with the whole blanched almonds and dark chocolate shards.

Stuffed Figs (recipe on page 213)

Brazos de Gitano

Gypsy's Arm Cake

Similar to a Swiss roll, this rich dessert, brazos de gitano, as it is known in Spain, is a favourite on feast days in Barcelona. For the full Spanish effect, try preparing it with Pedro Ximénez. A traditional Spanish postre that will leave you licking your lips!

200 g (7 oz) dark chocolate, broken into pieces
80 ml (2½ fl oz/⅓ cup) strong black coffee
7 eggs, at room temperature, separated
150 g (5½ oz/⅔ cup) caster (superfine) sugar
1 tablespoon icing (confectioners') sugar

2 tablespoons unsweetened cocoa powder
1 teaspoon rich sweet sherry, such as Pedro Ximénez or anís liqueur
300 ml (10½ fl oz) cream, for whipping

Preheat the oven to 180°C (350°F/Gas 4). Grease a 29 x 24 x 3 cm (11½ x 9½ x 1½ in) Swiss roll tin (jelly roll tin) and line with baking paper.

Melt the chocolate with the coffee in a heatproof bowl over a small saucepan of simmering water, stirring occasionally, until almost melted. Remove from the heat and stir until smooth. Set aside to cool a little.

Beat the egg yolks and caster sugar in a large bowl until light and creamy, then stir in the chocolate mixture. Whisk the egg whites in a separate bowl until soft peaks form. Using a large metal spoon or rubber spatula, gently fold the whites into the chocolate mixture. Pour into the lined tin and bake on the middle shelf of the oven for 15 minutes, or

until the cake springs back when lightly touched in the middle. Turn off the oven and open the door slightly.

After 10 minutes, turn out the cake onto a clean tea towel (dish towel) that has been dusted with the combined icing sugar and cocoa. Leave for 30 minutes, or until cool.

Sprinkle the top of the sponge with the sherry. Whip the cream and spread over the sponge. Roll the cake up, using the tea towel to help you but removing it as you go. Wrap in plastic wrap and refrigerate until ready to slice and serve.

SERVES 8–10

Right: Carefully and gently fold the egg whites into the rich chocolate mixture.

Far right: Spread the cream over the cake and roll up neatly.

PAN DE HIGOS

Fig Bread

The fig season is short, but during this time the fruit is plentiful (on the island of Majorca alone there are more than 80 varieties), so fig lovers have devised ways of making them last, one of the best of which is this rich spicy bread.

1 kg (2 lb 4 oz) dried figs, roughly chopped
200 g (7 oz/1½ cups) hazelnuts, roasted
300 g (10½ oz/2 cups) almonds, blanched and roasted
1 teaspoon ground cinnamon
2 tablespoons caster (superfine) sugar
½ teaspoon ground aniseed
½ teaspoon ground black pepper
¼ teaspoon ground cloves

85 g (3 oz) dark chocolate, melted (or substitute 3 tablespoons honey)
2 tablespoons anís liqueur (or other aniseed-flavoured liqueur such as Ouzo or Sambuca)
1 tablespoon finely grated lemon zest
300 g (10½ oz/2 cups) extra almonds, toasted and finely chopped

Put the chopped figs in a food processor and process until very finely chopped. Transfer to a large bowl. Chop or process the nuts until finely chopped. Add to the figs, along with remaining ingredients, except for the extra almonds. Mix thoroughly with your hands until combined.

Divide the mixture into four balls each. Roll these into cylinders about 20 cm (8 in) long and 5 cm (2 in) in diameter and place on to baking paper.

Roll each cylinder in the finely chopped almonds. Let them dry for a few hours and then wrap them individually in plastic wrap. Store in an airtight container in the refrigerator. These will keep for several months. When serving, slice into 1 cm (½ in) thick rounds and enjoy with coffee.

MAKES 4 ROLLS 20 CM X 5 CM

Far left: Clean hands make the best tools for combining the moist and dry ingredients.

Left: Roll the cylinders in the almonds, patting gently to help them stick.

Torrijas

Fried Bread with Honey

An impressive but simple-to-make dessert of Andalucían origin, associated with Semana Santa. This dessert is enriched by the addition of the sensational single-origin Spanish sweet sherry, Pedro Ximénez. Be sure to use a good-quality white bread.

4 thick slices of day-old bread
150–200 ml (5–7 fl oz) Pedro Ximénez or Malaga wine
60 ml (2 fl oz/¼ cup) vegetable oil
2 eggs, beaten with a dash of milk

1 teaspoon ground cinnamon
2 tablespoons caster (superfine) sugar, for dusting
honey, to serve (optional)

Dip both sides of the bread slices in the sherry, then drizzle on any remaining liquid. Leave to sit for a few minutes to absorb the sherry.

Heat the oil in a frying pan over medium heat. Dip the bread slices in the beaten egg, then fry on each side for 3–4 minutes, or until golden brown.

Drain the fried bread on paper towel, then dust with the combined cinnamon and sugar, and drizzle with honey, if using.

SERVES 4

Coat the slices of bread well in the egg mixture.

Helado de Turrón
Almond Turrón Ice Cream

Turrón, a nougat confection, is popular throughout Spain and a fantastic Christmas treat. This cool summer dessert is flavoured with turrón. Try to use Pedro Ximénez or muscatel sherry, perhaps drizzling some extra over the ice cream before serving.

TURRÓN
115 g (4 oz/½ cup) caster (superfine) sugar
50 g (1¾ oz/⅓ cup) whole blanched almonds, roasted

6 egg yolks
80 g (2¾ oz/⅓ cup) caster (superfine) sugar, extra
100 ml (3½ fl oz) sweet sherry, such as Pedro Ximénez or Malaga wine
435 ml (15¼ fl oz/1¾ cups) cream, for whipping

To make the almond turrón, combine the sugar and 60 ml (2 fl oz/¼ cup) of water in a saucepan. Stir over low heat with a metal spoon until the sugar has dissolved. Increase the heat, bring to the boil and cook for 6–8 minutes, or until the mixture is dark golden brown (but not burnt).

Scatter the almonds onto a greased baking tray, then pour on the toffee and set aside to harden.

Mix the egg yolks and extra sugar in a bowl with an electric beater until pale and creamy. Whisk in the sherry. Transfer the mixture to a heatproof bowl over a saucepan of simmering water, making sure the bowl does not touch the water. Whisk constantly for 10–15 minutes, or until the mixture is thick and foamy. Remove from the heat and cool slightly, then refrigerate until chilled.

Whip the cream until firm, but not stiff. Using a large metal spoon or spatula, gently fold the cream into the chilled custard until combined. Pour the mixture into a shallow metal container – a cake tin with a capacity of at least 1 litre (35 fl oz/4 cups) is ideal. Place in the freezer until frozen around the edges. Remove and beat with an electric beater until smooth. Return the custard to the container and re-freeze. Repeat this process three times, or until the ice cream is soft and not icy.

Crush the almond turrón and fold it through the ice cream after the final mixing.

For the final freezing, put the ice cream in an airtight container and place a sheet of greaseproof paper underneath the lid. Freeze for 3 hours, or until firm.

SERVES 6

Food Journey

LA PASTELERÍA

Travelling around Spain, you'll find that every town has its own special sweet — regional and seasonal pastries and cakes are to be had everywhere. Although they're not typically consumed after dinner, there is a rich tradition of sweets associated with fiestas and religious ceremonies.

Most importantly, there is turrón. Traditionally associated with Christmas, and possibly dating back even to pre-Roman times, these nutty honey-based nougats come in many forms, from soft turrón blando originating in Xixona, to hard turrón duro from Alicante, packed with almonds, and soft brown pan de Cadiz.

There is a class of flour-based sweet dishes, biscuits and buns: torta de Santiago from Santiago de Compostela; fried buñuelos; and feast-day classics such as brazos de gitano (Gypsy's arm roll) and light-as-cloud polvorones.

Eggs are used extensively as in the famed tocino de cielo (heavenly bacon), and the various yemas, candied egg-yolk recipes and the ancient huevo hilado, a sugared egg yolk in sweet thin threads.

In the cooler north, where milk is abundant, there are rich milk-based recipes such as leche frita (fried milk), a thick custard cut into squares and then fried, and a Spanish version of rice pudding, arroz con leche, as well as various sweet curds.

But it is the convents that are the repositories of some of the finest sweet dishes in the country, with an ancient tradition of confectionery and cakes. Today, some convents still make and sell pastries and cakes to the outside world often, like San Leandro, via a revolving door that requires no speech or contact.

As the Spanish don't tend to cook sweets in their homes, nor do traditional restaurants serve a wide range of desserts, if you're looking for something along those lines, stop off at one of the pastelerías and take your pick! The Spanish more commonly enjoy their pastries and sweets for breakfast and merienda rather than as after-dinner desserts.

SOPLILLOS GRANADINOS
Moorish Almond Meringues

This recipe, another enduring legacy from the Moorish occupation, is from Granada. They are also known as soplillos Alpujarreños, meringues from the Alpujarras, the lush green mountain range south of Granada. Simple and luscious.

150 g (5½ oz/¼ cup) slivered almonds, lightly toasted
3 egg whites
200 g (7 oz) caster (superfine) sugar

1 tablespoon lemon juice
1 teaspoon natural vanilla extract

Preheat the oven to 140°C (275°F/Gas 1). Line two baking trays with baking paper.

Place the almonds in a food processor and process until very finely ground.

Whisk the egg whites with electric beaters until firm peaks form. With the motor still running, gradually whisk in the sugar, then the lemon juice and vanilla – you should end up with a glossy, firm-peaked mixture.

Using a large metal spoon or a spatula, fold the ground almonds into the meringue mixture.

Either spoon or pipe the meringue onto the prepared trays and bake for 1 hour. Turn off the heat and leave in the oven until completely cooled. Store in an airtight container for up to two weeks.

MAKES ABOUT 24

Right: Whisk the sugar, lemon juice and vanilla into the egg white mixture until thick and glossy.

Far right: Spoon the meringue mixture onto the lined trays.

Tortas de Aceite y Anís

Aniseed Wafers

These popular and delicate olive oil wafers are flavoured with whole aniseeds, giving them a sweet licorice edge. They are good at any time of the day and make a delicious accompaniment to a carajillo, a Spanish specialty: short black coffee laced with anís.

375 g (13 oz/3 cups) plain (all-purpose) flour
125 ml (4 fl oz/½ cup) olive oil
125 ml (4 fl oz/½ cup) beer
60 ml (2 fl oz/¼ cup) Spanish anís liqueur

115 g (4 oz/½ cup) caster (superfine) sugar
40 g (1½ oz/¼ cup) sesame seeds
2 tablespoons aniseeds

Preheat the oven to 200°C (400°F/Gas 6). Lightly grease a baking tray and line with baking paper.

Sift the flour and 1 teaspoon salt into a large bowl and make a well. Add the olive oil, beer and anís and mix with a large metal spoon until the dough comes together. Transfer the dough to a lightly floured surface and knead for about 4 minutes, or until smooth. Divide the dough in half, then divide each half into eight portions.

In a small bowl, combine the sugar, sesame seeds and aniseeds.

Pile the seed mixture on a work surface. Roll out each portion of dough over the mixture to a 15 cm (6 in) round, embedding the seeds underneath. Put the rounds on a baking tray with the seeds on top. Bake for 5–6 minutes, or until the bases are crisp.

Put the wafers 10 cm (4 in) under a hot grill (broiler) for about 40 seconds, or until the sugar caramelizes and the surface is golden. Transfer to a wire rack to cool.

MAKES 16

Flan de Naranja

Orange Custard

The addition of orange makes this a refreshingly delicious variation on the old favourite, flan, the Spanish version of creme caramel. Often the only dessert on a Spanish restaurant menu (along with fruit and cheese), this is a delightful treat.

275 g (9¾ oz/1¼ cups) caster (superfine) sugar
200 ml (7 fl oz) fresh orange juice, strained

7 egg yolks, at room temperature
1 egg

Preheat the oven to 170°C (325°F/Gas 3). Lightly grease four 125 ml (4 fl oz/½ cup) ramekins or moulds with oil spray and place in a baking dish.

Put 80 g (2¾ oz/⅓ cup) of the sugar and 60 ml (2 fl oz/¼ cup) of water in a small saucepan and stir gently over low heat until the sugar dissolves. Increase the heat to a low boil and cook for about 10 minutes, or until the mixture becomes golden and smells like caramel. Quickly divide the toffee among the ramekins and tilt to cover the bases. Set aside.

Put the orange juice and remaining sugar in a small saucepan over low heat and stir gently until the sugar dissolves. Increase the heat, bring to the boil and cook for 2 minutes, or until the mixture is slightly syrupy. Leave to cool for 10 minutes.

Put the egg yolks and whole egg in a bowl and beat with a wooden spoon. Pour the cooled orange juice onto the eggs, stirring until well combined. Pass the mixture through a sieve, then pour into the moulds and place them in a small baking dish.

Pour enough boiling water into the baking dish to come halfway up the side of the ramekins. Bake for 15 minutes, then carefully remove the ramekins from the water and cool to room temperature. Chill completely in the refrigerator (this will take about 3 hours).

When ready to serve, dip the moulds in hot water for 10 seconds, then invert onto serving plates.

SERVES 4

Right: Work quickly to ensure the base of each ramekin is covered with the toffee before it sets.

Far right: Boil the orange juice mixture until slightly syrupy.

Bizcochos Borrachos

Drunken Cakes

This is another way to treat the Spanish sponge cake. Cut the sponge into single-serve chunks and make the cake 'drunk' (borracho) by soaking it in Malaga wine, sherry or other rich, sweet Spanish liqueur, like Licor 43, flavoured with vanilla and orange.

1 bizcocho (see page 210), baked in a square or
   rectangular tin
115 g (4 oz/ ½ cup) caster (superfine) sugar

125 ml (4 fl oz/ ½ cup) Malaga wine
ground cinnamon, for dusting (optional)
whipped cream, to serve

Cut the cooled bizcocho into squares.

Put the sugar and 125 ml (4 fl oz/ ½ cup) of water in a small saucepan over low heat and stir with a metal spoon until the sugar has dissolved. Bring to the boil and cook for 4 minutes. Add the wine and boil for 3 minutes, or until syrupy.

Drizzle the syrup evenly over the cake squares. Dust the tops with cinnamon, if using, and serve with whipped cream.

SERVES 8–10

Far left: Add the sweet wine to the water and sugar mixture.

Left: Cook the mixture until it is syrupy before drizzling over the sponge cake squares.

TORTA DE SANTIAGO

Almond Torte

Since medieval times the Galician city of Santiago de Compostela has been the destination for millions of pilgrims who have walked the pilgrim's trail, starting from either Navarra or southern France. At the end of their journey, this cake awaits them.

450 g (1 lb/2½ cups) whole blanched almonds, lightly roasted
150 g (5½ oz) unsalted butter, softened
400 g (14 oz) caster (superfine) sugar
6 eggs, at room temperature

150 g (5½ oz) plain (all-purpose) flour, sifted
2 teaspoons grated lemon zest, very finely chopped
2 tablespoons lemon juice
icing (confectioners') sugar, for dusting

Preheat the oven to 170°C (325°F/Gas 3). Lightly grease a 24 cm (9½ in) spring-form cake tin. Finely grind the almonds in a food processor.

Using electric beaters, cream the butter and sugar in a bowl until light and fluffy. Add the eggs one at a time, beating well after each addition. Using a large metal spoon, fold in the flour, ground almonds and chopped lemon zest. Stir until all the ingredients are just combined.

Pour the batter into the prepared tin and bake for 1 hour 20 minutes, or until a skewer inserted in the centre comes out clean. Cool for 5 minutes, then brush the top with lemon juice until it has all been absorbed. Transfer to a wire rack and cool completely. Dust with icing sugar – in a cross pattern, using a stencil if you wish.

SERVES 8

Use a paper stencil for a neat icing sugar cross.

PERAS EN VINO TINTO

Pears Cooked in Red Wine

Catalan cuisine loves to take advantage of the quality fruit that comes from the Pyrenees, as here in this classic dish, which has escaped the confines of its borders. Now found all around the Spanish peninsula, it makes a sumptuous end to any meal.

4 firm, ripe pears, peeled and cored
80 ml (2½ fl oz/⅓ cup) lemon juice
250 ml (9 fl oz/1 cup) dry red wine

2 cinnamon sticks
220 g (7¾ oz/1 cup) sugar
8 slices lemon

Rub the pears with the lemon juice. Put the red wine, cinnamon sticks, sugar, lemon slices and 250 ml (9 fl oz/1 cup) water in a saucepan over low heat and simmer gently until the sugar has dissolved. Bring to the boil, then reduce the heat and simmer for 15 minutes. Add the pears and simmer for a further 20 minutes, carefully turning occasionally to ensure even colouring. Leave the pears to soak in the syrup overnight, if possible.

Remove the pears from the syrup and set aside. Simmer the syrup over high heat for 15 minutes, or until it thickens slightly.

Serve the pears whole, drizzled with the syrup.

SERVES 4

When the syrup thickens, it is ready to coat the pears.

Arroz con Leche

Rice Pudding

A dish popular in many regions of the globe, rice pudding is also a dish beloved by generations of Spaniards, both young and old. Here the dish is given an Iberian zing with the addition of orange zest and cinnamon – a bow to the Moors.

1 litre (35 fl oz/4 cups) milk
220 g (7 3/4 oz/1 cup) paella or short-grain rice
1 large strip orange zest
1 cinnamon stick

1 teaspoon natural vanilla extract
145 g (5 oz/2/3 cup) caster (superfine) sugar
orange zest, to garnish (optional)

Put the milk, rice, orange zest, cinnamon, vanilla, sugar and a pinch of salt in a large saucepan and stir over high heat until the sugar has dissolved. Allow to just come to the boil, then reduce the heat to a simmer.

Cook the rice mixture over low heat, stirring regularly, for 50 minutes, or until the rice is tender but not mushy. Stirring not only helps

to ensure the rice mixture does not stick to the bottom of the pan, it also helps to produce a very creamy texture.

Remove the orange zest and cinnamon stick from the pan with tongs. Serve the rice pudding warm or cold, garnished with thin strips of orange zest.

SERVES 6

TOCINO DE CIELO

Heaven's Bacon

Translated as 'bacon from heaven', this is a popular Andalucían recipe, often made by the nuns in their convents. It is indeed heavenly, but also satisfyingly wicked. It is traditionally decorated with tiny meringues, which sit on the top.

285 g (10 oz/1¼ cups) caster (superfine) sugar
1 vanilla bean, split

1 egg
6 egg yolks

Preheat the oven to 180°C (350°F/Gas 4). Put 120 g (4¼ oz/½ cup) of the sugar in a small saucepan with 2 tablespoons water. Stir with a metal spoon over low–medium heat until all the sugar has dissolved. Bring to the boil and cook for a further 10 minutes, or until the toffee is a rich golden colour. Remove the pan from the heat and, taking care not to burn yourself, pour into a 20 cm (8 in) square cake tin, tilting to cover the base of the tin.

Meanwhile, put 250 ml (9 fl oz/1 cup) water in a saucepan with the vanilla bean and remaining sugar. Stir until the sugar has dissolved. Bring to the boil, then reduce the heat and simmer for 10 minutes, or until the liquid has reduced to a slightly syrupy consistency. Leave to cool a little. Remove the vanilla bean.

Using electric beaters, beat the whole egg and egg yolks until smooth. Slowly add a stream of the cooled sugar and vanilla mixture while beating on high speed. Once combined, strain the liquid onto the toffee mixture in the cake tin.

Put the cake tin in a larger baking dish. Pour enough boiling water into the larger dish to come one-third of the way up the side of the cake tin. Bake for 35–40 minutes, or until just set. Cool slightly and then refrigerate until cold.

When ready to serve, dip the tin into a hot water bath for 30 seconds to loosen the caramel. Run a knife around the custard and unmould onto a serving plate. Drizzle any remaining caramel over the top and cut into small squares to serve.

MAKES ABOUT 18 PIECES

Far left: Beat the cooled sugar and vanilla mixture into the eggs.

Left: Strain the egg mixture onto the toffee mixture that has set in the tin.

LECHE FRITA

Fried Milk

One of the more traditional desserts, this recipe can be found all over Spain (especially in the north). Marrying cinnamon and vanilla, it can be fussy to make the first time, but is well worth the effort – especially if cooking for children.

500 ml (17 fl oz/2 cups) milk
1 cinnamon stick
1 strip lemon zest, 5 x 1 cm (2 x ½ in)
1 vanilla bean, split
140 g (5 oz) unsalted butter
250 g (9 oz/2 cups) plain (all-purpose) flour
145 g (5 oz/⅔ cup) caster (superfine) sugar

4 eggs, separated
125 g (4½ oz/1¼ cups) dry breadcrumbs
vegetable oil, for shallow-frying
1 teaspoon ground cinnamon mixed with 80 g
   (2¾ oz/⅓ cup) caster (superfine) sugar,
   for dusting

Grease a 27 x 17 cm (11 x 6½ in) rectangular tin and line the base and long sides with baking paper. Put the milk, cinnamon stick, lemon zest and split vanilla bean in a saucepan and bring to the boil. Turn off the heat.

Melt the butter in a large heavy-based saucepan over medium heat. Stir in 185 g (6½ oz/1½ cups) of the flour. The mixture will form a loose clump around your spoon. Reduce the heat to low and stir for 30 seconds, then stir in the sugar. Strain the warm milk into the pan a little at a time, stirring constantly. Mix for about 10 minutes, or until a smooth mass forms and it leaves the side of the pan. Remove from the heat and stir in the egg yolks one at a time, beating well after each addition (the mixture should now be quite glossy).

Spread the custard mixture in the tin, smoothing the surface with your hand. Set aside for 1 hour to cool and set.

Lightly whisk the egg whites together. Lift the set custard from the tin and carefully cut into 5 cm (2 in) squares. Dip in the remaining flour to coat all sides. Dip into the egg whites and then into the breadcrumbs. Set aside.

Pour the oil into a large frying pan to a depth of 1 cm (½ in). Heat the oil, add a few squares at a time and cook for about 1 minute per side, or until browned. Drain on paper towel and dust all over with the cinnamon and sugar mixture while still hot. Serve straight away.

SERVES 4–6

Basics

*An important step in mastering any cuisine is learning
the basic recipes and techniques. Straight from the recipe journal,
here are the ones no Spanish cook would be without.*

TOMATES PELADOS
Peeled Tomatoes

ripe tomatoes

Score a cross in the base of each tomato with a knife. Put the tomatoes in a bowl of boiling water for 10 seconds, then plunge into a bowl of cold water. Remove from the water and peel the skin away from the cross – it should slip off easily. If desired, remove the seeds with a teaspoon, and chop the flesh.

PIMIENTOS ASADOS
Roasted Capsicums

capsicums (peppers)

Cut each capsicum (pepper) into four flattish pieces and remove the seeds and white membrane. Arrange the pieces, skin-side up, in a single layer on a baking tray. Cook under a hot grill (broiler) until the skins are blackened and blistered.

Put the capsicums in a large bowl and cover with plastic wrap (or put them in a plastic bag), then leave to cool for 10 minutes.

Peel away the blackened skins from the capsicums and cut the flesh into thin strips.

ALLIOLI

Garlic Mayonnaise

The original of this Catalan classic was simply made with garlic and olive oil. Today, egg yolks are added, but it should still be strongly garlic in flavour and smooth and white in texture. Perfect with seafood and potatoes.

2 egg yolks
4 garlic cloves, crushed

60 ml (2 fl oz/¼ cup) white wine vinegar or lemon juice
250 ml (8 fl oz/1 cup) mild olive oil

Put the egg yolks, garlic and half of the vinegar or lemon juice in a bowl. Using a balloon whisk, or electric beaters, whisk until well combined. While you continuously whisk, gradually add the oil in a slow stream until you have a thick mayonnaise. If at some point the mayonnaise becomes too thick, add the remaining vinegar and continue adding the rest of the oil. Season well.

Allioli will keep in an airtight container in the refrigerator for 2–3 days.

MAKES ABOUT 250 ML (9 FL OZ/1 CUP)

GLOSSARY

ANISEED (also known as anise or anise seed)
These greenish-brown, licorice-flavoured seeds are used in both sweet and savoury cooking and also to make anís, an alcoholic beverage similar to schnapps. Buy the seeds whole because once ground, they lose flavour.

BACALAO
The Spanish term for salt cod that has been salted and dried. It must be soaked for about 20 hours before use to rehydrate the fish and to remove the excess salt. Once prepared, the bacalao flakes easily and is popular in fritters, but is also cut into larger pieces for poaching, simmering or baking in various sauces.

BAY LEAVES
Glossy green leaves sold fresh or dried and used to add a strong, slightly peppery flavour to wet savoury dishes and occasionally to puddings and custards. The fresh leaves are a little stronger than the dried.

BESAN (CHICKPEA FLOUR)
A high-protein flour made by finely grinding chickpeas. Chickpea flour has a nutty flavour and is ideal for making batter for deep-fried foods and for thickening sauces.

CALASPARRA RICE (also known as paella rice)
A medium-grained, high-quality absorbent white rice grown in the Calasparra region that is traditionally used to make paella. Bomba is one variety of Calasparra rice and can sometimes be found labelled as such.

CAPER BERRIES
The fruit of the caper bush, which appear after the flowers. They are usually preserved in brine and are often served as an accompaniment or garnish (much like olives).

CAPERS
The small flowers of the caper bush, which are preserved in brine and sometimes just salt. They should be rinsed well before use. They have a piquant flavour and are used in small amounts in dressings, salads and as a garnish. The smaller the caper, the more aromatic and therefore expensive.

CAVA
A quality Spanish sparkling white wine made by the same bottle fermentation method as Champagne. Cava is refreshing to drink, and can be used to make sweet and savoury sauces.

CAYENNE (also known as cayenne pepper)
A powder made from ground red chilli peppers native to South America. It is very pungent and spicy and should be used sparingly. It is often added to wet dishes for heat and is sometimes sprinkled over cheese-topped dishes before baking or grilling (broiling) as the flavours are complementary.

CHICKPEAS
Small legumes commonly used in rustic, home-style cooking. Pale brown or yellow in colour, they are commonly available dried and need to be soaked and cooked before being consumed; however, you can now find them already prepared and tinned for convenience.

Once soaked, or after the initial boiling, chickpeas should be rubbed between your hands and rinsed to help remove their skins.

CHILLIES
Available fresh, dried or roasted, chillies belong to the capsicum (pepper) family and are native to South and Central America, from where they were taken by the Spanish and Portuguese into the Mediterranean. There are many different varieties of chilli and they vary dramatically in size, heat and flavour. The seeds and inner membranes of the chillies should be removed if less heat is desired.

CHORIZO
The best known of all Spanish sausages, chorizo is made from minced (ground) or chopped pork and pork fat, flavoured with sweet and hot paprika (pimentón), garlic and black pepper. Sometimes sold soft for cooking in wet dishes (such as soups or stews), it is more commonly found as a hard, cured sausage that can be eaten as is, but is often sliced and fried, then eaten as a snack or added to wet dishes.

CUMIN (sometimes known as cummin)
Indigenous to the east Mediterranean region, the seeds are used whole or ground to flavour savoury dishes and breads. The pungent, slightly nutty flavour is enhanced by dry-roasting it before use.

JAMÓN
Spanish ham, resembling good-quality prosciutto, is available in different grades and varies in flavour and texture, depending on its region of origin. Jamón Ibérico is ham from the black Iberian pigs, which are fed mainly on acorns, figs and sometimes olives, giving the meat great flavour and aroma. The ham is salted, air-dried and then matured for about two years. Jamón serrano, or mountain ham, is from the fattened white pigs of the Sierra Nevada region, which are salted, and then air-cured for at least a year. Jamón is extremely flavoursome and tender and is often added to cooked dishes or eaten on its own.

MANCHEGO CHEESE
One of Spain's most famous cheeses, originally made from the milk of Manchego sheep from the La Mancha region. A semi-firm cheese with a rich but mellow flavour, which alters with age. Sold as fresh, semi-cured and cured – the texture firming and flavour deepening at each of these stages. It is perfect for everyday eating and has wonderful melting properties.

MORCILLA
A northern Spanish sausage made from pig's blood, similar to black pudding. It is very rich and often spiced with cinnamon, cloves and nutmeg. Some variations include rice, potato, garlic, white beans, onion or fennel. They are boiled before being hung up to dry and are then sometimes also smoked. Often added to stews or casseroles or sautéed and crumbled into stuffings and dishes such as scrambled eggs.

NAVY BEANS (also known as haricot beans or pea beans)
One of the many members of the haricot bean family, navy beans are small white legumes sold dried, and are perfect for soups and stews as they require long, slow cooking. If not available, other members of the haricot bean family can be substituted, such as cannellini, pinto or borlotti (cranberry) beans.

PAPRIKA (PIMENTÓN)
Small red capsicums (peppers) varying in heat from mild to hot are dried, sometimes smoked, then ground for use in savoury dishes both for flavour and colour. The rusty red powder is most commonly sold as sweet or mild (dulce), medium hot (agridulce) and hot (picante). Smoked paprika is also popular in certain regions of Spain and a small amount adds a distinctive smoky flavour to savoury foods.

PIMIENTO/PIMIENTOS DEL PIQUILLO

Pimientos are a type of red capsicum (pepper). Pimientos del piquillo are small, hot, red capsicum, which are preserved in oil in a tin or jar after being roasted and charred, then carefully peeled. Ready for use, the whole pimiento del piquillo can be stuffed and then deep-fried or baked in sauce, or chopped and added to salads or other dishes. Pimiento can also be puréed to form the basis of a sauce or soup. Small amounts of the red pimiento are used to stuff green olives.

SAFFRON

The orange–red stigma of one species of the crocus plant is the most expensive spice in the world due to the fact that one flower contains only three stigmas, which are laboriously hand picked and then dried. Fortunately, only a little is needed when cooking. Sold in both thread and powdered form, beware of cheap imitations. Saffron is best toasted, then soaked in warm liquid for a few minutes before use – this helps to bring out the flavour and colour.

SQUID INK (also known as cuttlefish ink)

Used to colour and flavour Spanish rice dishes and sauces for seafood. The black ink is stored in a sac that can be removed from whole squid and cuttlefish but is also available in sachets from fishmongers or good delicatessens. It has a subtle savoury flavour that is not at all fishy, as one might expect.

TOCINO

Spanish fat bacon that is salted and air-cured but not smoked. Often sold covered with a layer of crystalline salt. It is used in stews and soups and, when made from Iberian pigs, is much sought after.

VINE LEAVES

Large green leaves of the grape vine are used in Mediterranean and Middle Eastern cookery, mainly to wrap foods before grilling (broiling), roasting or simmering. Commonly available in brine in jars, tins or packets, they are also sometimes sold fresh (these should be blanched in hot water until pliable before use). Vine leaves in brine should be rinsed or briefly soaked in cold water to remove the salty brine.

INDEX

Published in 2010 by Murdoch Books Pty Limited

Murdoch Books Australia
Pier 8/9, 23 Hickson Road
Millers Point NSW 2000
Phone: +61 (0)2 8220 2000
Fax: +61 (0)2 8220 2558
www.murdochbooks.com.au

Murdoch Books UK Limited
Erico House, 6th Floor
93–99 Upper Richmond Road
Putney, London SW15 2TG
Phone: +44 (0)20 8785 5995
Fax: +44 (0)20 8785 5985
www.murdochbooks.co.uk

Publisher: Lynn Lewis
Senior Designer: Heather Menzies
Series Design Concept: Sarah Odgers
Photographer: Alan Benson, Natasha Milne, Ashley Mackevicus,
Prue Roscoe, Ian Hofsetter and Martin Brigdale
Project Editor: Justine Harding
Designer: Susanne Geppert
Index: Jo Rudd

ISBN: 978-1-74266-107-0

PRINTED IN CHINA.

IMPORTANT: Those who might be at risk from the effects of salmonella poisoning (the elderly, pregnant women, young children
and those suffering from immune deficiency diseases) should consult their doctor with any concerns about eating raw eggs.

OVEN GUIDE: You may find cooking times vary depending on the oven you are using. For fan-forced ovens, as a general rule,
set the oven temperature to 20°C (35°F) lower than indicated in the recipe.